Ernesto cira

Advanced Penetrating Testing: Mastering Advanced Penetration Techniques for Robust Defense and Resilient Systems

Contents

1.

2.

   1.

   2.

   3.

3.

   1.

   2.

4.

   1.

   2.

   3.

5.

   1.

   2.

   3.

6.

   1.

Preface

In the ever-expanding landscape of cyberspace, the stakes have never been higher. As our world becomes increasingly interconnected, the need for robust cybersecurity measures is paramount. It is within this dynamic and challenging realm that "Advanced Penetration Testing" finds its purpose.

This book offers a road map for people who want to learn the art and science of ethical hacking. It offers a tour through the complicated dance between attackers and defenders, as well as a thorough guidebook for those who are ready to push the boundaries of standard penetration testing.

Embarking on a Journey of Mastery

The art of penetration testing goes beyond the basics. It delves into the intricacies of advanced scanning techniques, vulnerability analysis, and exploitation strategies. With every chapter, readers will unlock the secrets of post-exploitation, privilege escalation, and the subtle nuances of social engineering. Once considered impenetrable, wireless networks will reveal their vulnerabilities and the world of mobile applications and cloud security will be laid bare.

A Holistic Approach to Cybersecurity

"Advanced Penetration Testing" takes a holistic approach, addressing the challenges posed by emerging technologies such as IoT and blockchain. The book doesn't just stop at identifying vulnerabilities; it equips readers with the tools and knowledge to fortify their defences. As we navigate through real-world case studies, ethical hacking becomes not just a skill but a mindset—one that places responsibility, ethics, and a commitment to securing digital landscapes at its core.

Practical Insights, Real-world Scenarios

Each chapter contains a wealth of practical ideas, as well as real-world examples that bridge the gap between theory and practice. This book appeals to both novices looking for a strong foundation and seasoned experts looking to keep ahead of the curve, covering everything from the foundations to cutting-edge approaches.

The Future of Cybersecurity Awaits

The last chapters of this book discuss cybersecurity's difficulties and future directions as we stand at the vanguard of technological innovation. We consider the ramifications of artificial intelligence and machine learning, foresee the hazards posed by future technologies, and prepare for the ever-changing world of digital threats.

For Whom This Book Is Written

Whether you are a cybersecurity enthusiast, an IT professional, or an ethical hacker aiming to sharpen your skills, "Advanced Penetration Testing" invites you to embark on a transformative journey. This isn't just a book; it's a guide that empowers you to navigate the complex cybersecurity web with confidence and mastery.

Welcome to a world where knowledge is power, and mastery is within your reach. Let the journey begin.

Chapter 1: Introduction to Advanced Penetration Testing

What is Advanced Penetration Testing?

A complex and in-depth technique to evaluate the security of computer systems, networks, apps, and other IT environments is referred to as advanced penetration testing. Penetration testing, often known as ethical hacking, is the practice of simulating cyber assaults to detect and exploit flaws in a system's defences. The label "advanced" denotes a greater degree of experience, procedures, and technologies utilized in the testing process.

The following are important components of Advanced Penetration Testing:

1. **Comprehensive Evaluations**: Advanced penetration testing goes beyond simple vulnerability detection. It entails a detailed review of an organization's security posture, including network security, online applications, mobile devices, wireless networks, and other areas.

2. **Advanced Penetration Testers Utilize a Wide Range of Advanced Tools and Methods:** Advanced penetration testers utilize a wide range of advanced tools and methods to

detect and exploit vulnerabilities. This might include the use of bespoke scripts, advanced penetration testing frameworks, and even the creation or modification of exploits.

3. **Real-World Simulation:** The goal of advanced penetration testing is to mimic real-world cyber threats. Testers frequently imitate malicious actors' tactics, methods, and procedures (TTPs), including advanced persistent threats (APTs).

4. **Beyond technological vulnerabilities**, sophisticated penetration testing sometimes involves social engineering evaluations. This entails attempting to influence someone into exposing sensitive information or conducting inappropriate acts to test an organization's human factors.

5. **Post-Exploitation Analysis:** Advanced penetration testing includes detailed post-exploitation analysis in addition to detecting vulnerabilities. Examining the effect of successful exploits, estimating the possibility for lateral movement within a network, and comprehending the overall risk to the enterprise are all part of this process.

6. **Approaches That Are Tailored:** Advanced penetration testing is not a one-size-fits-all technique. Testers customize their techniques to the target environment's particular traits and technology. This may entail developing bespoke exploits or employing customized tactics for certain systems.

7. **Continuous Improvement:** Advanced penetration testing is an essential component of any security plan. The results of these tests are used by organizations to constantly enhance their security policies. This might include changing

regulations, deploying new technology, and giving more staff training.

8. **Considerations for Legal and Ethical Compliance:**
    Advanced penetration testing is always carried out within the confines of a legal and ethical framework. Testers must receive clear authorization from the entity being tested, and testing must follow local and international laws and regulations.

Evolution of penetration testing:

The evolution of penetration testing shows how this cybersecurity activity has evolved and transformed over time. Penetration testing, often known as ethical hacking, is a proactive strategy for finding and correcting security flaws in computer systems, networks, applications, and other IT infrastructure.

1. **Early Stages (Pre-Internet Era):**

   - In the early days of computing, security concerns were not as prominent as they are today.

   - Penetration testing, if conducted at all, was more ad-hoc and often limited to physical security assessments.

2. Growth with the Internet:

- The widespread adoption of the Internet in the 1990s brought about new security challenges.

- Organizations began to recognize the need for systematic testing to identify and mitigate vulnerabilities in their online presence.

3. Regulatory Compliance and Standards:

- The late 1990s and early 2000s saw the introduction of various regulations and standards that mandated security assessments for certain industries.

- Examples include the Payment Card Industry Data Security Standard (PCI DSS) for the payment card industry.

4. Professionalization and Certification:

- As the demand for skilled security professionals increased, the field of penetration testing became more formalized.

- Professional certifications, such as Certified Ethical Hacker (CEH) and Offensive Security Certified Professional (OSCP), emerged to validate the skills of ethical hackers.

5. Advancements in Tools and Techniques:

- The 2000s and 2010s witnessed significant advancements in penetration testing tools and techniques.

- Automated scanners, exploit frameworks, and other tools became integral to penetration testing methodologies.

6. Shift to Continuous Testing:

- Traditional penetration testing was often a point-in-time assessment. However, with the rise of continuous integration and continuous deployment (CI/CD) practices, there was a shift towards continuous security testing.

- Organizations began to embrace more frequent and iterative testing to keep up with the rapidly changing threat landscape.

7. Cloud and Mobile Security:

- The proliferation of cloud computing and mobile technologies introduced new attack surfaces and security challenges.

- Penetration testing methodologies expanded to cover cloud security and mobile application security.

8. Focus on Advanced Threats:

- With the rise of advanced persistent threats (APTs) and sophisticated cyberattacks, penetration testing evolved to simulate more targeted and persistent attack scenarios.

- Red teaming, which simulates realistic and sophisticated attacks, gained popularity.

9. Integration of AI and Machine Learning:

- The integration of artificial intelligence (AI) and machine learning (ML) into cybersecurity tools has influenced penetration testing.

- AI/ML is used for anomaly detection, pattern recognition, and improving the efficiency of security assessments.

10. **Globalization and Outsourcing:**

- As organizations expanded globally and embraced outsourcing, penetration testing became essential for assessing the security of third-party vendors and partners.

11. **Comprehensive Risk Assessments:**

- Modern penetration testing is not only about identifying technical vulnerabilities but also understanding the broader risk landscape.

- Social engineering assessments, physical security testing, and comprehensive risk assessments are now common components of penetration testing engagements.

Importance of advanced techniques:

1. **Complexity of Modern Systems:**

- As technology advances, systems become more complex, incorporating various layers of security. Advanced techniques are necessary to identify and exploit vulnerabilities in intricate and multifaceted environments.

2. **Sophistication of Cyber Attacks:**

- Cyber attackers continually enhance their methods, using more advanced and creative tactics. To effectively defend against these sophisticated attacks, penetration testers must employ advanced techniques that replicate the evolving threat landscape.

3. Identification of Zero-Day Vulnerabilities:

- Advanced techniques are crucial for identifying and exploiting zero-day vulnerabilities—security weaknesses that are unknown to the system vendor or the cybersecurity community. Penetration testers must possess the skills to discover and assess these vulnerabilities before malicious actors do.

4. Defense Against APTs:

- Advanced Persistent Threats (APTs) are long-term, targeted attacks often conducted by well-funded and organized adversaries. Penetration testers need advanced techniques to simulate APT scenarios, helping organizations understand and defend against these persistent and sophisticated threats.

5. Comprehensive Security Assessments:

- Advanced techniques enable penetration testers to conduct more thorough security assessments. This includes testing not only network and application vulnerabilities but also aspects like social engineering, physical security, and emerging technologies.

6. Adapting to New Technologies:

- The technology landscape is dynamic, with the emergence of new technologies such as IoT, cloud computing, and AI. Penetration testers must stay current and develop advanced skills to assess the security of these technologies effectively.

7. Realistic Simulations:

- Advanced techniques contribute to creating realistic and challenging simulations during penetration testing. This is crucial for organizations to understand how their defences perform under sophisticated attack scenarios, helping them improve their security posture.

8. Legal and Ethical Considerations:

- Advanced penetration testing often involves more intricate scenarios, and testers must be well-versed in the legal and ethical aspects of their work. This includes obtaining proper authorization, ensuring compliance with regulations, and adhering to ethical standards while conducting tests.

9. Continuous Learning and Improvement:

- The field of cybersecurity is constantly evolving, and professionals must engage in continuous learning to stay ahead. Advanced techniques reflect a commitment to ongoing education and skill development, ensuring that penetration testers are well-equipped to face emerging threats.

Chapter 2: Planning and Preparation

Understanding the scope of penetration testing:

Understanding the breadth of penetration testing is crucial to building a comprehensive and effective security assessment. Penetration testing, often known as ethical hacking in the field of cybersecurity, is a proactive way to detect vulnerabilities and flaws in a system, network, or application. The scope of penetration testing outlines the assessment's boundaries and objectives, ensuring that the testing process is focused, targeted, and aligned with the goals of the company. Both the penetration testing team and the company commissioning the test require this expertise.

The scope of penetration testing defines what will be tested, how deep the testing will go, and the rules of engagement. It is a strategic decision-making process that entails specifying the assets to be tested, the testing methodologies to be used, and the allowable scope of simulated assaults. Organizations may optimize resource consumption, control risks, and get useful insights into their security posture by defining a defined scope.

Identifying the assets to be tested is the first step in determining the scope of penetration testing. This entails compiling a list of the organization's systems, networks, apps, and other digital assets. The scope might cover a narrow subset of assets, such as a web application, or it can include the complete IT infrastructure. Asset identification is critical because it ensures that the testing team focuses on the areas that are most relevant to the security issues of the firm.

Once the assets have been identified, the next step in establishing the scope is to decide on the testing methodologies to be used. Network penetration testing, application penetration testing, wireless network testing, and social engineering assessments are all examples of penetration testing. The testing methodologies used are determined by the organization's objectives, the nature of its assets, and the unique dangers it confronts. A financial organization, for example, may prioritize evaluating the security of its online banking application, whereas a manufacturing firm may prioritize testing the security of its industrial control systems.

Furthermore, the scope should define the acceptable scope of the simulated assaults. This entails defining the rules of engagement, which explain the parameters and limits of the penetration testing operations. Rules of engagement may include concerns such as testing timeframes, testing hours, communication procedures, and the testing team's ability to simulate real-world threats. Established rules of engagement aid in the prevention of disruptions to regular company operations and the reduction of the danger of unexpected effects.

Understanding the extent of penetration testing entails thinking about other forms of testing, such as black-box testing, white-box testing, and grey-box testing. The testing team has no prior knowledge of the internal systems and infrastructure during black-box testing. This mimics an external attacker's perspective and gives information into how effectively an organization's defences can survive real-world threats. In contrast, white-box testing entails giving the testing team with complete knowledge of the internal systems, including source code and architectural information. This method enables a more in-depth examination of internal security systems. Grey-box testing creates a compromise between black-box and white-box testing by giving the testing team partial knowledge.

The significance of having a well-defined scope cannot be emphasized. A penetration test may lack direction if there is no clear knowledge of what is in scope and what is out of scope, spending time and resources on areas that are not vital to the organization's security posture. In contrast, an extremely narrow scope may result in the organization neglecting possible vulnerabilities and leaving itself vulnerable to real-world dangers.

Information gathering and reconnaissance:

1. **Information Gathering**:

- **Passive Information Gathering:** This involves collecting data without directly interacting with the target. It includes researching publicly available information, such as WHOIS databases, DNS records, social media profiles, and other open-source intelligence (OSINT) techniques. The idea is to gather as much information as possible without alerting the target.

- **Active Information Gathering**: In this phase, the tester starts interacting directly with the target to gather more detailed information. Techniques include network scanning, port scanning, and fingerprinting to identify active hosts, services, and operating systems. This phase may also involve searching for vulnerabilities related to the identified services.

2. **Reconnaissance**:

- **Network Reconnaissance**: This involves mapping out the target's network infrastructure, and identifying IP addresses, subnets, and network devices. Tools like Nmap or Nessus can be used for network scanning to discover hosts and open ports.

- **Application Reconnaissance**: Focusing on the target's web applications and services, this phase aims to identify potential vulnerabilities or weaknesses. Testers may use tools like Burp Suite for web application scanning or other specialized tools for specific services.

- **Social Engineering Reconnaissance:** This involves gathering information about individuals within the target organization. This can include employee names, roles, and contact details. Social engineering attacks often leverage this information to trick individuals into providing sensitive information.

- **Physical Reconnaissance**: In cases where physical security is relevant, testers may gather information about the target's physical premises. This could include details about security systems, access points, and potential entry points.

3. **Documentation**:
   - **Creating a Reconnaissance Report:** Throughout the information gathering and reconnaissance phases, it's essential to document all findings systematically. This documentation serves as a reference for the penetration tester and can be crucial when preparing the final penetration testing report.

4. **Analysis and Planning**:
   - **Analyzing Collected Information:** Once the initial information is gathered, the penetration tester analyzes the data to identify potential vulnerabilities, weak points, and areas of interest. This analysis informs the testing strategy for subsequent phases.

- **Planning the Attack:** Based on the analysis, the penetration tester develops a plan for the active testing phases. This plan outlines the specific tests and techniques that will be used to identify and exploit vulnerabilities. It also includes considerations for the scope and rules of engagement.

Chapter 3: Advanced Scanning Techniques

Network scanning:

Network scanning is an important step in the penetration testing and network security process. It entails the methodical finding of devices, systems, and services on a network. The basic goal of network scanning is to obtain topological information, identify active hosts, and discover open ports and services. This data is useful for determining the network's structure and potential weaknesses.

The following are the most important components of network scanning:

1. **Host Discovery**:
   - **Ping Sweeps**: This involves sending ICMP Echo Request (ping) messages to a range of IP addresses to determine which hosts are alive and responsive.
   - **TCP/UDP Scans**: Using tools like Nmap, a tester can send TCP or UDP packets to various ports on a target host to determine if they are open or closed.

2. **Port Scanning:**

- **TCP Connect Scans**: Attempts to establish a full TCP connection with the target port.

- **SYN/Stealth Scans**: Initiates a connection but doesn't complete it, useful for evading intrusion detection systems.

- **UDP Scans**: Identifies open UDP ports and services.

- **Service Version Detection**: Determines the version and type of service running on an open port.

3. **Network Mapping:**

- Identifies the layout and structure of the network, including routers, switches, and subnets.

- Tools like Nmap can provide visual representations of the network topology.

4. **OS Fingerprinting**:

- Determines the operating system of a target host by analyzing the characteristics of network packets.

- Helps attackers tailor their exploits to vulnerabilities specific to the identified OS.

5. **Banner Grabbing**:

- Retrieves information from banners or responses provided by services running on open ports.

- Helps in identifying software versions and potentially vulnerable applications.

6. **Vulnerability Scanning**:

- Some network scanning tools incorporate vulnerability databases to identify known vulnerabilities associated with open ports and services.

7. **Continuous Monitoring**:

- Network scanning is not a one-time activity. Regular scans help in monitoring changes in the network, identifying new devices, and ensuring ongoing security.

8. **Stealth and Evasion Techniques**:

- Testers may use techniques like slow scanning, decoy scanning, or fragmented packet scanning to avoid detection by intrusion detection systems.

Host discovery:

Host discovery is an important step in the network reconnaissance and penetration testing process. The basic purpose of host discovery is to detect and map active network devices (hosts). Understanding the network's topology, possible vulnerabilities, and attack surface begins with knowing which hosts are live and reachable. Here are some typical approaches for discovering hosts:

1. **Ping Sweeps:**

   - **ICMP Echo Requests (Ping):** This is a common method where the tester sends ICMP Echo Request packets to a range of IP addresses. Live hosts respond with an ICMP Echo Reply. However, some firewalls and hosts may be configured to ignore or block ICMP traffic.

2. **TCP/UDP Scans:**

   - **TCP SYN Scan:** This involves sending TCP SYN packets to various ports on a target host. Live hosts respond with a TCP SYN-ACK if the port is open, indicating the host is reachable.

   - **UDP Scan:** Some hosts may not respond to TCP SYN packets, but they might respond to UDP packets. A UDP scan involves sending UDP packets to different ports to identify open ports and active hosts.

3. **ARP Scanning:**

   - **Address Resolution Protocol (ARP) Scan:** ARP is used to map an IP address to a physical MAC address. By sending ARP requests to a range of IP addresses, a tester can identify which IP addresses are associated with live hosts on the local network.

4. **DNS Interrogation:**

   - **DNS (Domain Name System) Query:** By querying DNS servers for information about a domain, a tester can identify the IP addresses associated with active hosts. This is particularly useful when testing external networks or web applications.

5. Service Banner Grabbing:

- **Banner Grabbing:** Involves connecting to open ports on a target host and capturing the banner information sent by the service running on that port. This can reveal the type of service and sometimes even the version, helping in host identification.

6. Network Scanning Tools:

- Various automated tools like Nmap, Angry IP Scanner, and others provide comprehensive host discovery features. These tools often combine multiple techniques, making the discovery process more efficient.

7. Wireless Network Scanning:

- In the context of wireless networks, tools like NetStumbler or Kismet can be used to discover active wireless hosts by monitoring the wireless spectrum for beacon frames.

Service enumeration:

Service enumeration is an important step in the penetration testing and cybersecurity assessment process. It entails detecting and identifying network services that are active on target systems. The purpose is to collect data about the services, their versions, and settings. This information is critical for evaluating potential vulnerabilities in these services and planning further stages of the penetration test.

The following are the most important features of service enumeration:

1. **Port Scanning**:

   - The first step in service enumeration is often port scanning. Port scanning involves sending network packets to a target system to discover open ports. Each open port is associated with a specific service or application. Common tools for port scanning include Nmap, Nessus, and Masscan.

2. **Banner Grabbing**:

   - Once open ports are identified, the next step is banner grabbing. This involves connecting to the open ports and capturing the "banner" or response from the service running on that port. The banner often includes information about the service, such as its name and version. Banner grabbing can be done using tools like Telnet, Netcat, or specialized banner-grabbing tools.

3. **Service Version Detection**:

   - Determining the version of a service is crucial for understanding potential vulnerabilities associated with that version. Many vulnerabilities are version-specific, and attackers often target known vulnerabilities. Tools like Nmap can automatically detect service versions based on their responses and provide detailed information about the identified services.

4. **Protocol Analysis:**

- In addition to discovering standard services like web servers (HTTP), FTP, or SSH, service enumeration also involves identifying less common or proprietary protocols. Understanding these protocols is essential for a comprehensive assessment of the target environment.

5. **Enumerating Information**:

- Gathering additional information about the services, such as user accounts, available resources, and configurations. This may involve querying services for specific information or using techniques like SNMP (Simple Network Management Protocol) enumeration.

6. **Automated Tools and Scripts**:

- Penetration testers often use automated tools and scripts to streamline the service enumeration process. These tools can quickly identify open ports, grab banners, and provide detailed reports. However, manual verification is essential to ensure the accuracy of the   results.

Chapter 4: Vulnerability Analysis

Vulnerability assessment methodologies:

Vulnerability assessment is a crucial component of cybersecurity that involves identifying, quantifying, and prioritizing vulnerabilities in a system, network, or application. The goal is to assess the security posture and potential risks associated with the target environment. Here are some common vulnerability assessment methodologies:

1. **Asset Identification**:
   - Identify and document all assets within the organization, including hardware, software, networks, and data repositories.
   - Categorize assets based on their criticality to business operations.

2. **Threat Modeling**:
   - Analyze potential threats and risks to the organization.
   - Consider various attack vectors and scenarios that could be exploited by malicious actors.

3. **Vulnerability Scanning**:

- Use automated tools to scan networks, systems, and applications for known vulnerabilities.

- Regularly update vulnerability databases to ensure the latest threats are covered.

4. **Penetration Testing:**

- Conduct controlled, simulated attacks to identify vulnerabilities that may not be detected by automated tools.

- Penetration testing goes beyond scanning and involves attempting to exploit vulnerabilities to assess the real-world impact.

5. **Manual Testing**:

- Engage security experts to perform manual testing and analysis, often using a combination of automated tools and human expertise.

- Manual testing can uncover subtle vulnerabilities that automated tools might overlook.

6. **Security Code Review:**

- Examine the source code of applications to identify security vulnerabilities.

- This methodology is particularly relevant for web applications and software development projects.

7. **Configuration Review**:

- Assess the security configurations of systems, networks, and devices.

- Ensure that security settings are in line with industry best practices and organizational security policies.

8. **Patch Management**:

- Regularly review and update systems and applications with the latest security patches.

- Establish a robust patch management process to address known vulnerabilities promptly.

9. **Compliance Audits:**

- Evaluate systems and processes against industry standards, regulations, and compliance requirements.

- Ensure that security controls are in place to meet legal and regulatory obligations.

10. **Risk Assessment:**

- Evaluate the potential impact and likelihood of exploitation for each identified vulnerability.

- Prioritize vulnerabilities based on risk, considering factors such as business impact and the likelihood of exploitation.

11. **Continuous Monitoring**:

- Implement continuous monitoring systems to detect and respond to new vulnerabilities as they emerge.

- Leverage intrusion detection systems and security information and event management (SIEM) tools.

12. **Documentation and Reporting**:

- Document all findings, including vulnerabilities, their potential impact, and recommended remediation strategies.

- Provide clear and actionable reports to stakeholders, including IT teams and management.

Automated vs. manual vulnerability analysis:

Automated and human vulnerability analysis are two methodologies used in cybersecurity to find and analyze potential security flaws in a system, application, or network. Each method has advantages and disadvantages, and they are frequently used in tandem to offer a full security evaluation.

Automated Vulnerability Analysis:

1. **Definition**:

- Automated vulnerability analysis involves the use of software tools and scanners to identify security vulnerabilities automatically.

- These tools are designed to detect known vulnerabilities based on a database of signatures, patterns, or behaviours associated with security issues.

2. **Advantages**:

- **Efficiency**: Automated tools can quickly scan large networks or codebases, making them efficient for handling large-scale assessments.

- **Consistency**: Automated tools apply the same criteria consistently, reducing the likelihood of human error.

- **Regular Scanning**: They can be scheduled for regular scans, ensuring continuous monitoring for new vulnerabilities.

3. **Limitations**:

- **False Positives/Negatives**: Automated tools may produce false positives (identifying a vulnerability that doesn't exist) or false negatives (missing a real vulnerability).

- **Limited Context Understanding**: They may lack the ability to understand the context in which a system operates, potentially leading to inaccurate assessments.

4. **Use Cases**:

- Best suited for routine, repetitive scanning tasks.
- Initial identification of common vulnerabilities.
- Continuous monitoring for known threats.

Manual Vulnerability Analysis:

1. **Definition**:

- Manual vulnerability analysis involves human experts actively reviewing and analyzing systems, applications, or code to identify security vulnerabilities.

- This approach requires a deep understanding of system architecture, application logic, and security principles.

2. **Advantages**:

- **Contextual Understanding**: Human analysts can understand the unique context of a system, allowing them to identify complex and context-dependent vulnerabilities.

- **Identification of Emerging Threats:** Analysts can identify novel vulnerabilities that automated tools might overlook, especially in the case of zero-day vulnerabilities.

3. **Limitations**:

- **Resource-Intensive**: Manual analysis is time-consuming and may not be feasible for large-scale assessments.

- **Subject to Human Error**: Human analysts can make mistakes, and the consistency of findings may vary among different analysts.

4. **Use Cases:**

- In-depth analysis of critical systems or applications.

- Identifying complex, context-dependent vulnerabilities.

- Penetration testing and ethical hacking exercises.

Best Practices:

- **Combination Approach**: Many organizations adopt a hybrid approach, using automated tools for initial scans and manual analysis for in-depth inspection.

- **Regular Updates**: Automated tools should be regularly updated with the latest vulnerability signatures to stay current.

- **Expertise**: Manual analysis requires skilled security professionals with a deep understanding of the systems being assessed.

Common vulnerabilities and exposures (CVEs):

Common Vulnerabilities and Exposures (CVEs) is a method for identifying, naming, and referencing publicly known cybersecurity flaws. The objective of CVEs is to make it simpler to understand and remedy vulnerabilities by facilitating data exchange among diverse vulnerability capabilities (tools, databases, and services). Here's an explanation of the most important components of CVEs:

1. **Identification and Naming:**

- **CVE Identifier**: Each vulnerability is assigned a unique identifier known as a CVE ID. This identifier takes the form "CVE-

YYYY-NNNN" where YYYY is the year of assignment, and NNNN is a sequential number.

2. **Publicly Known Vulnerabilities**:
   - **Public Database**: CVEs are catalogued in a publicly accessible database maintained by the MITRE Corporation. This database is freely available and widely used by the cybersecurity community.
   - **Public Disclosure**: For a vulnerability to receive a CVE ID, it must be publicly disclosed. This means that information about the vulnerability is made available to the public, either by the vendor, the security researcher who discovered it, or another party.

3. **Standardization:**
   - **Common Language:** CVE provides a common language for discussing and sharing information about vulnerabilities. This standardization is crucial for effective communication among security professionals, vendors, and the wider community.

4. **Cross-Referencing:**
   - **Linking to Other Databases**: CVE entries often include references to other databases or resources that provide additional information about the vulnerability, such as the National Vulnerability Database (NVD) or vendor-specific security advisories.

5. Impact Assessment:

- **Severity Scores:** CVE entries may include severity scores or ratings to help organizations assess the potential impact of a vulnerability on their systems.

- **Common Vulnerability Scoring System (CVSS):** The CVSS is often used to quantify the severity of vulnerabilities, taking into account factors like exploitability, impact on confidentiality, integrity, and availability.

6. Interoperability:

- **Integration with Security Tools**: Many cybersecurity tools and products use CVEs to identify and classify vulnerabilities. This allows for better interoperability between different security solutions.

7. Updates and Corrections:

- **CVE Updates:** The CVE system is dynamic, and entries can be updated or corrected as more information becomes available or as the status of a vulnerability changes.

- **Retirement of CVE IDs**: If a vulnerability is later determined not to exist or was incorrectly assigned a CVE ID, the ID may be retired to avoid confusion.

8. Community Involvement:

- **Collaboration:** CVE involves collaboration between various stakeholders, including security researchers, vendors, and organizations that use the information to secure their systems.

Chapter 5: Exploitation Techniques

Exploitation frameworks and tools:

Exploit frameworks and tools are critical components of penetration testing and ethical hacking. Security experts use them to detect and exploit vulnerabilities in computer systems, networks, and applications. The major purpose of employing these tools is to imitate real-world cyber assaults, assisting enterprises in identifying and correcting security flaws before bad actors can exploit them. An overview of exploitation frameworks and tools is provided below:

Exploitation Frameworks:

1. **Metasploit:**

   - **Description**: Metasploit is one of the most popular and widely used exploitation frameworks. It provides a comprehensive set of tools for penetration testing, including exploits, payloads, and auxiliary modules.

   - **Features**:

   - Exploit development and testing.

   - Payload generation for various operating systems.

   - Post-exploitation modules for maintaining access.

2. **ExploitDB:**

   - **Description**: Exploit Database (ExploitDB) is an online platform that provides a large collection of exploits, shellcodes, and security-related resources. While not a framework in itself, many penetration testers use exploits from ExploitDB within their testing methodologies.

3. **Canvas:**

   - **Description**: Canvas is a commercial exploitation framework designed for penetration testers and security professionals. It offers a user-friendly interface and a variety of exploits for different platforms.

4. **Cobalt Strike:**

   - **Description**: Cobalt Strike is a commercial, full-featured penetration testing tool that includes an exploitation framework. It is often used for post-exploitation activities and has capabilities for social engineering and reporting.

Exploitation Tools:

1. **Nmap (Network Mapper):**

   - **Description**: Nmap is primarily a network scanning tool, but it also includes scripting capabilities that allow security professionals to develop custom scripts for exploitation purposes. It's often used during the initial reconnaissance phase.

2. SQLMap:

- **Description**: SQLMap is a powerful open-source tool specifically designed for detecting and exploiting SQL injection vulnerabilities in web applications. It automates the process of identifying and exploiting these vulnerabilities.

3. Burp Suite:

- **Description**: Burp Suite is a web application security testing tool. While its main focus is on web application scanning, it includes features for identifying and exploiting vulnerabilities such as cross-site scripting (XSS) and cross-site request forgery (CSRF).

4. Hydra:

- **Description**: Hydra is a password-cracking tool that supports various network protocols. It is commonly used for brute-force attacks against services like FTP, SSH, and HTTP.

5. BeEF (Browser Exploitation Framework):

- **Description**: BeEF is a penetration testing tool focused on exploiting web browser vulnerabilities. It allows testers to assess the security of a target by leveraging client-side vulnerabilities in web browsers.

6. OWASP ZAP (Zed Attack Proxy):

- **Description**: ZAP is an open-source security testing tool designed for finding vulnerabilities in web applications. It includes automated scanners and various tools for identifying and exploiting web-related security issues.

Considerations:

- **Ethical Use**:

Exploitation tools and frameworks should only be used for ethical hacking and penetration testing with proper authorization. Unauthorized use can lead to legal consequences.

- **Stay Updated:**

Security professionals should keep these tools and frameworks updated to ensure they have the latest exploits and improvements.

- **Documentation**:

Proper documentation of the exploitation process is crucial for reporting and remediation purposes. This includes detailing the steps taken, vulnerabilities exploited, and recommendations for mitigation.

Buffer overflow attacks:

A buffer overflow is a sort of software vulnerability that happens when a program writes more data to a memory block, or buffer than it was originally allocated for. This overflow can damage or overwrite nearby memory, resulting in unforeseen effects like as crashes, unpredictable behaviour, or even uncontrolled code execution.

A more extensive discussion of buffer overflow attacks may be found here:

1. **Buffer and Memory Layout**:

   - Programs often use buffers to store data temporarily. These buffers are allocated in a program's memory.

   - Memory is organized into regions, such as the stack and heap. The stack, for instance, is used for storing local variables and function call information.

2. **Vulnerability Introduction**:

   - When a program does not properly check the size of the data it receives or does not ensure that it fits within the allocated buffer, a buffer overflow vulnerability is introduced.

   - Attackers take advantage of this vulnerability by providing input that exceeds the bounds of the buffer.

3. **Overflowing the Buffer**:

   - The attacker sends more data than the buffer can hold, causing the excess data to overflow into adjacent memory regions.

4. **Overwriting Data:**

- The overflowed data can overwrite crucial information, such as return addresses, function pointers, or other variables.

- Overwriting these values can lead to the manipulation of a program's control flow.

5. **Exploiting Control Flow**:

- By carefully crafting the overflowed data, an attacker can manipulate the program's control flow to redirect it to malicious code.

- This could involve overwriting a function's return address with the address of the attacker's code, which is typically injected into the program.

6. **Execution of Arbitrary Code**:

- Once control flow is redirected to the attacker's code, the attacker can execute arbitrary commands or payloads.

- This could lead to the compromise of the entire system, unauthorized access, or other malicious activities.

Buffer overflow attacks can be directed at a variety of programs, including applications, operating systems, and network protocols. They are a severe security risk and have previously been responsible for several security flaws and exploits.

Secure coding standards are critical for preventing buffer overflow attacks. This involves input validation, correct bounds checking, and the use of safe coding approaches such as employing functions that handle buffer bounds checking automatically (for example,'strncpy' instead of 'strcpy' in C). Furthermore, current programming languages and tools frequently incorporate features and protections to protect against buffer overflow problems.

Web application attacks:

Online application assaults are hostile operations that target online applications to exploit vulnerabilities in the code, configuration, or logic of the program. These attacks can lead to unauthorized access to sensitive information, service disruptions, and other security concerns. Web applications are widely utilized for a variety of functions, such as online banking, e-commerce, social networking, and others, making them appealing targets for attackers.

Here are some examples of popular web application attacks:

1. **SQL Injection (SQLi):**

   - **Description:** SQL injection occurs when an attacker injects malicious SQL code into input fields or parameters of a web application. This can lead to unauthorized access, data manipulation, and even deletion of the database.

   - **Prevention**: Use parameterized queries, input validation, and least privilege principles.

2. Cross-Site Scripting (XSS):

- **Description**: XSS involves injecting malicious scripts (usually JavaScript) into web pages that are then viewed by other users. This can lead to the theft of session cookies, defacement of websites, or other malicious actions.

- **Prevention**: Input validation, output encoding, and the use of secure coding practices.

3. Cross-Site Request Forgery (CSRF):

- **Description**: CSRF tricks a user's browser into performing unwanted actions on a web application where the user is authenticated. This can lead to actions being performed without the user's knowledge or consent.

- **Prevention**: Use anti-CSRF tokens, ensure that sensitive actions require authentication, and implement secure coding practices.

4. Command Injection:

- **Description:** Command injection occurs when an attacker injects malicious commands into a system command that is executed by the web application. This can lead to unauthorized access or execution of arbitrary commands on the server.

- **Prevention**: Avoid using user input in commands, implement proper input validation, and use parameterized commands.

5. Security Misconfigurations:

- **Description**: Security misconfigurations happen when a web application or its components are not securely configured. This can include default credentials, unnecessary services running, and overly permissive permissions.

- **Prevention**: Regular security audits, following security best practices, and minimizing the attack surface.

6. File Inclusion Vulnerabilities:

- **Description**: File inclusion vulnerabilities occur when an application allows an attacker to include files on a server through user-controllable input. This can lead to the execution of arbitrary code.

- **Prevention**: Avoid using user input directly in file inclusion operations, validate and sanitize input, and use secure coding practices.

7. Unvalidated Redirects and Forwards:

- **Description**: This occurs when a web application allows users to be redirected to external URLs without proper validation. Attackers can use this to redirect users to malicious sites.

- **Prevention**: Validate and sanitize user input for redirection, use safe redirects, and avoid using user input to construct URLs.

8. Insecure Direct Object References (IDOR):

- **Description**: IDOR occurs when an application provides access to objects based on user-supplied input. Attackers can manipulate this input to access unauthorized data.

- **Prevention**: Implement proper access controls, validate user permissions, and avoid exposing sensitive information in URLs.

43

Chapter 6: Post-Exploitation and Privilege Escalation

Maintaining access:

In the context of penetration testing and ethical hacking, maintaining access refers to the phase in which a penetration tester aims to establish a lasting presence on the target system after successfully exploiting a vulnerability. The goal is to maintain continuous access to the system for additional investigation, data exfiltration, or surveillance while avoiding detection by the system's security systems.

The following are critical factors for retaining access:

1. **Backdoors and Rootkits:**

- **Backdoors**: These are secret entry points or methods of bypassing normal authentication or encryption in a computer system. Penetration testers may install backdoors to maintain access.

- **Rootkits**: These are sets of software tools used by an attacker to hide the presence of other software or processes on a system.

Rootkits can be employed to maintain access while remaining undetected.

2. **Persistence Mechanisms**:

- Once initial access is achieved, the penetration tester aims to establish mechanisms that ensure persistence even if the system undergoes updates, reboots, or security patches.

- Common techniques include modifying system configurations, adding scheduled tasks, or inserting malicious code into startup scripts.

3. **Privilege Escalation**:

- The penetration tester might attempt to escalate their privileges on the compromised system to gain higher-level access, allowing them to control more resources and execute more commands.

4. **Tunneling and Pivoting**:

- Techniques like tunnelling and pivoting involve creating encrypted pathways or using compromised systems as intermediaries to access other parts of the network, extending the tester's reach beyond the initially compromised system.

5. **Anti-Forensic Measures**:

- To avoid detection, penetration testers may employ anti-forensic techniques, making it more difficult for security professionals to trace their activities on the compromised system.

6. **Monitoring and Stealth**:

- Penetration testers need to monitor their access points while remaining discreet. This involves understanding and evading security monitoring systems, such as intrusion detection systems (IDS) and antivirus software.

7. **Documentation**:

- It is crucial for ethical hackers to document the steps taken during the penetration test, including details about maintaining access. This documentation serves not only as a record for the tester but also as a resource for organizations to understand and address vulnerabilities.

Privilege escalation techniques:

A sort of cyberattack in which an unauthorized user acquires higher-level access or rights than they are meant to have is known as privilege escalation. This is an important stage for attackers since it lets them access sensitive information, execute instructions, and do operations that are normally banned. Privilege escalation may happen at many different levels, including local system privileges, network access, and even administrator privileges. Here are a few examples of frequent privilege escalation techniques:

1. **Exploiting Vulnerabilities:**

- **Operating System Vulnerabilities:** Attackers may exploit known vulnerabilities in the operating system to elevate their privileges. This could involve exploiting a flaw in the kernel or a system service.

- **Application Vulnerabilities**: Vulnerabilities in applications or services running on the system can also be exploited for privilege escalation. This might involve exploiting a flaw in a web server, database, or other software.

2. **Misconfigured Permissions**:

- **File and Directory Permissions**: If files, directories, or binaries have incorrect permissions, an attacker might be able to modify or replace them with malicious counterparts, leading to privilege escalation.

- **Sudo and Privilege Escalation through Script**s: Misconfigured sudoers files or scripts executed with elevated privileges can be exploited by attackers.

3. **Weak Authentication**:

- **Brute Force Attack**s: If an attacker can obtain or crack passwords, they may use them to gain unauthorized access and escalate their privileges.

- **Password Sniffing**: Monitoring network traffic for plaintext passwords can be used to obtain credentials and escalate privileges.

4. **Kernel Exploits**:

- **Kernel-Level Exploits**: Attackers may attempt to exploit vulnerabilities in the operating system's kernel to gain control over the entire system.

5. **DLL Hijacking and Dynamic Link Libraries**:

- **DLL Injection**: On Windows systems, attackers might use DLL (Dynamic Link Library) injection techniques to load malicious code into the address space of a running process, potentially leading to privilege escalation.

6. **Scheduled Tasks and Cron Jobs**:

- **Abusing Scheduled Tasks**: If a system executes scheduled tasks or cron jobs with elevated privileges, attackers may manipulate these tasks to escalate their privileges.

7. **Registry Manipulation (Windows)**:

- **Registry Privilege Escalation**: Manipulating Windows Registry settings may provide unauthorized users with elevated privileges.

8. **Abusing Service Permissions:**

- **Service Exploitation**: If a service is running with elevated privileges and has vulnerabilities, attackers might exploit those vulnerabilities to escalate their privileges.

9. **Exploiting Weak Service Configurations:**

- **Weak Configuration Files:** Poorly configured services or applications may expose opportunities for privilege escalation. This could include misconfigured service accounts or insecure settings.

10. **Physical Access:**

- **Direct Access to Hardware**: If an attacker has physical access to a system, they might use techniques such as booting from external media to gain elevated privileges.

Post-exploitation tools and tactics:

The phase of a cybersecurity assault in which an unauthorized entity has acquired access to a system or network and strives to keep that access, elevate privileges, and gather important information is referred to as post-exploitation. During this phase, post-exploitation tools and methods are used to maximize the impact of the attack and achieve the attacker's aims. Here are some of the most important components of post-exploitation tools and tactics:

1. Maintaining Access:

- **Backdoors and Shells:** Attackers often deploy backdoor programs or shell access to ensure they can re-enter the system even if the initial point of entry is discovered and closed.

- **Persistence Mechanisms**: Techniques like registry modifications, scheduled tasks, or service installation help attackers maintain access across system reboots.

2. Privilege Escalation:

- **Exploiting Vulnerabilities**: Attackers may search for and exploit vulnerabilities that allow them to escalate their privileges from a low-privileged user to an administrator.

- **Password Cracking**: If the attacker has obtained password hashes, they might use tools to crack weak passwords and gain access to higher-privileged accounts.

3. Credential Harvesting:

- **Keyloggers**: Capture and log keystrokes to obtain usernames and passwords.

- **Credential Dumping**: Extract stored credentials from the system, often from memory or databases.

4. Lateral Movement:

- **Exploiting Trust Relationships**: Use compromised credentials or vulnerabilities to move laterally within the network, accessing other systems and resources.

- **Pass-the-Hash (PtH)**: Utilize stolen password hashes to authenticate to other systems without knowing the actual passwords.

5. **Data Exfiltration**:

- **Compression and Encryption**: Compress and encrypt stolen data before exfiltrating it to avoid detection.

- **Covert Channels**: Use covert channels to hide data within seemingly innocuous network traffic.

6. **Covering Tracks:**

- **Log Manipulation**: Delete or modify log entries to erase evidence of the attacker's activities.

- **Anti-forensic Tools**: Use tools designed to counter forensic analysis and make it more difficult for investigators to trace the attacker's actions.

7. **Evasion Techniques**:

- **Polymorphic Malware**: Constantly change the code of malware to evade signature-based detection.

- **Traffic Manipulation**: Alter the characteristics of network traffic to avoid detection by intrusion detection systems.

8. **Information Gathering**:

- **System Enumeration**: Collect detailed information about the compromised system, including hardware, software, and network configurations.

- **User and Group Information**: Gather details about users and groups to aid in further exploitation.

9. **Remote Administration**:

- **Remote Desktop Protocols**: Use tools that allow remote desktop access to control systems from a distance.

- **Command and Control (C2) Servers**: Establish communication channels with remote servers to control compromised systems.

10. **File and Directory Operations**:

- **File Upload/Download**: Transfer files to and from the compromised system.

- **File and Directory Listing**: Enumerate and list files and directories on the target system.

Chapter 7: Wireless Network Penetration Testing

Wi-Fi security:

Wireless network security is critical for protecting wireless networks from unwanted access, data breaches, and other security risks. Here are some important components of Wi-Fi security:

1. **Encryption Protocols:**
   - **WEP (Wired Equivalent Privacy):** Considered insecure and easily cracked, it is not recommended for use.
   - **WPA (Wi-Fi Protected Access)**: Introduced as a replacement for WEP, it has various versions (WPA, WPA2, WPA3). WPA2 is widely used and provides stronger security.
   - **WPA3**: The latest standard, offering enhanced security features and protection against brute-force attacks.

2. **Authentication Methods:**
   - **Pre-Shared Key (PSK)**: Commonly used in home networks where users enter a passphrase to access the network.

- **Enterprise Mode:** In larger networks, typically used in business settings, users are authenticated individually through a central server using methods like RADIUS.

3. SSID (Service Set Identifier) Broadcasting:

- **Hidden SSID:** Some networks choose not to broadcast their SSID, thinking it adds an extra layer of security. However, this is not foolproof and can be easily discovered.

4. MAC Address Filtering:

- **Whitelisting:** Only allowing specific devices (MAC addresses) to connect to the network. While this provides some control, it can be bypassed through MAC spoofing.

5. Intrusion Detection and Prevention Systems (IDPS):

- Implementing systems that can detect and prevent unauthorized access. This includes monitoring for unusual patterns and behaviours.

6. VPN (Virtual Private Network):

- Using VPNs for secure communication over untrusted networks, including public Wi-Fi. This encrypts the data traffic between the device and the network.

7. Regular Security Audits and Penetration Testing:

- Conducting regular security audits and penetration tests to identify vulnerabilities and weaknesses in the network.

8. **Firmware and Software Updates:**

   - Keeping Wi-Fi routers and access points updated with the latest firmware and security patches to protect against known vulnerabilities.

9. **Strong Passwords:**

   - Using strong, unique passwords for Wi-Fi networks to prevent unauthorized access. Avoid using default passwords provided by manufacturers.

10. **Guest Network:**

   - Setting up a separate guest network with restricted access to the main network to enhance security.

11. **Firewall Configuration:**

   - Configuring firewalls on routers and access points to filter incoming and outgoing traffic and prevent unauthorized access.

12. **Physical Security:**

   - Ensuring physical security of networking equipment to prevent unauthorized individuals from gaining physical access to the devices.

WPA/WPA2 cracking:

WPA (Wi-Fi Protected Access) and WPA2 are wireless computer network security technologies. They were designed to be more secure than the previous and less secure WEP (Wired Equivalent Privacy) protocol. WPA and WPA2 employ better encryption techniques to prevent unwanted access to Wi-Fi networks.

Cracking WPA/WPA2 is attempting to get unwanted access to a protected Wi-Fi network by exploiting security protocol weaknesses. It should be noted that trying to break a Wi-Fi network without specific permission is both illegal and unethical. Only with sufficient authority should penetration testing or ethical hacking be performed.

Here are some important elements of WPA/WPA2 cracking:

1. Authentication and Key Management:
   - WPA/WPA2 uses a 4-way handshake process for authentication and key management between the client device (such as a laptop or smartphone) and the access point (Wi-Fi router).
   - During this handshake, a pre-shared key (PSK) or passphrase is used to derive encryption keys.

2. Common Attack Methods:
   - **Brute Force Attacks:** Involves systematically trying all possible combinations of passwords until the correct one is found. This method is time-consuming and resource-intensive, especially if strong, complex passwords are used.

- **Dictionary Attacks:** Uses a pre-compiled list of potential passwords (a dictionary) to try to match against the hashed password. This is more efficient than brute force but still requires significant computing power.

3. **Rainbow Tables:**

- Rainbow tables are precomputed tables containing the hash values for many possible passwords. Attackers can use these tables to quickly look up the hashed value of a known password, thereby speeding up the cracking process.

4. **WPS (Wi-Fi Protected Setup) Vulnerabilities:**

- Some attacks exploit vulnerabilities in the WPS feature, a simplified method for adding devices to a network. If WPS is enabled and poorly configured, it can be susceptible to brute force attacks.

5. **Offline Cracking:**

- Attackers often capture the WPA/WPA2 handshake data between the client and the access point. They can then use offline cracking tools to attempt to recover the pre-shared key from this captured data.

6. **Countermeasures**:

- Using a strong, complex passphrase or key makes brute force and dictionary attacks more difficult.
- Regularly updating Wi-Fi equipment firmware and software can patch known vulnerabilities.

- Disabling WPS if it's not needed can prevent attacks that exploit WPS weaknesses.

Wireless network attacks:

Wireless network assaults are security breaches that target wireless network weaknesses. These attacks make use of flaws in the design of wireless protocols and encryption techniques, allowing unwanted network access or jeopardizing the confidentiality and integrity of transmitted data. Here are some examples of frequent wireless network attacks:

1. **Wireless Eavesdropping (Passive Attacks):**
   - **Description:** Attackers passively monitor and capture wireless network traffic without actively participating in the communication.
   - **Purpose**: To gather sensitive information such as login credentials or confidential data.
   - **Countermeasures**: Encryption protocols like WPA3, VPNs, and monitoring tools to detect unusual network activity.

2. **Wireless Interception (Active Attacks)**:
   - **Description**: Attackers actively intercept and modify wireless communications between devices.

- **Purpose**: Modify or manipulate data, inject malicious content, or impersonate legitimate network entities.

- **Countermeasures**: Strong encryption, secure protocols, and intrusion detection/prevention systems.

3. Wireless Spoofing:

- **Description:** Attackers impersonate a legitimate wireless access point (AP) to trick devices into connecting to a malicious network.

- **Purpose**: Capture sensitive information, perform man-in-the-middle attacks, or distribute malware.

- **Countermeasures**: Use strong authentication methods (e.g., WPA2/WPA3), implement secure configurations, and educate users about connecting only to trusted networks.

4. Evil Twin Attacks:

- **Description**: Attackers set up a rogue wireless access point with a name (SSID) similar to a legitimate network to lure users into connecting.

- **Purpose**: Intercept traffic, capture login credentials, or deploy phishing attacks.

- **Countermeasures**: Vigilant monitoring for rogue APs, user education, and secure network configurations.

5. **Denial-of-Service (DoS) and Distributed Denial-of-Service (DDoS):**

- **Description:** Attackers flood the wireless network with a high volume of traffic or deauthenticate legitimate users, rendering the network unavailable.

- **Purpose**: Disrupt network services, cause system instability, or create a distraction for other attacks.

- **Countermeasures**: Intrusion prevention systems, rate limiting, and traffic filtering.

6. **WPS (Wi-Fi Protected Setup) Attacks:**

- **Description**: Exploiting vulnerabilities in WPS, attackers attempt to gain unauthorized access by brute-forcing the PIN or exploiting implementation flaws.

- **Purpose**: Gain access to the Wi-Fi network without knowing the pre-shared key.

- **Countermeasures**: Disable WPS if not needed, use strong, unique passwords, and keep firmware up to date.

7. **Rogue Device Attacks:**

- **Description**: Unauthorized devices connect to the wireless network, potentially posing security risks.

- **Purpose**: Gain network access, launch attacks, or eavesdrop on communications.

- **Countermeasures**: Network monitoring, MAC address filtering, and regular security audits.

Chapter 8: Social Engineering and Physical Security

Social engineering tactic:

Attackers utilize social engineering to persuade individuals to disclose personal information, execute activities, or make security blunders. Unlike traditional hacking approaches, which focus on technological flaws, social engineering makes use of human psychology to get access to sensitive information. Here are some examples of frequent social engineering techniques:

1. Phishing:

   - **Email Phishing**: Attackers send deceptive emails that appear to be from a trustworthy source, such as a bank or a colleague, to trick individuals into providing sensitive information like passwords or credit card details.

   - **Spear Phishing**: This is a targeted form of phishing where the attacker customizes their messages for a specific individual or organization, often using personal information to increase credibility.

2. Impersonation:

- **Authority Figures**: Attackers may impersonate authority figures, such as IT personnel, to convince individuals to share sensitive information or perform actions that compromise security.

- **Company Employees**: Impersonating a coworker or someone within the organization to gain access to information or systems.

3. Baiting:

- Attackers leave physical devices, such as infected USB drives or malware-laden CDs, in places where they are likely to be found. Curious individuals who pick up and use these devices unknowingly install malware on their systems.

4. Quizzes and Surveys:

- Attackers create fake quizzes, surveys, or contests, often shared through social media or email, to collect personal information. People may unknowingly provide details that can be used for password recovery or other malicious purposes.

5. Pretexting:

- Attackers create a fabricated scenario or pretext to engage with individuals and extract sensitive information. This could involve posing as a co-worker, contractor, or service provider to gain trust and access.

6. **Pharming**:

   - Attackers use malicious websites or DNS spoofing to redirect individuals to fake websites that appear legitimate. This tactic aims to collect sensitive information, such as login credentials.

7. **Tailgating**:

   - Also known as "piggybacking," this tactic involves an unauthorized person physically following an authorized individual into a restricted area. This is common in office settings where access is controlled by key cards or badges.

8. **Quid Pro Quo:**

   - Attackers offer a service or assistance in exchange for sensitive information. For example, an attacker might pose as IT support and offer to help with a computer issue, gaining access to the system in the process.

9. **Elicitation**:

   - Extracting information through casual conversation or interviews. Attackers may pose as researchers, reporters, or even friendly strangers to gather information that can be used in a social engineering attack.

10. **Reverse Social Engineering:**

   - Instead of the attacker initiating contact, the victim is manipulated into seeking out the attacker. This could involve creating a situation where the victim believes they need help or assistance.

Physical security assessments:

Physical security audits are an important part of penetration testing and security auditing. They entail assessing an organization's physical safeguards and controls in place to secure sensitive information, assets, and persons. The purpose is to uncover physical security infrastructure weaknesses that might be exploited by an adversary. The following are major elements of physical security assessments:

1. **Perimeter Security:**
   - **Fencing and Gates**: Evaluate the effectiveness of physical barriers like fences and gates in preventing unauthorized access.
   - **Access Control Points**: Assess the security of entry and exit points, such as doors and gates, including the use of access control systems.

2. **Building Security**:
   - **Doors and Locks**: Inspect the strength and integrity of doors and locks to prevent unauthorized entry.
   - **Windows:** Check the security of windows to ensure they are resistant to forced entry.

- **Alarms and Sensors**: Evaluate the deployment and effectiveness of alarm systems and sensors.

3. Surveillance Systems:

- **CCTV Cameras**: Assess the placement and coverage of surveillance cameras to monitor and record activities.
- **Monitoring Stations:** Check the security of monitoring stations and the procedures for reviewing footage.

4. Security Personnel:

- **Guard Force:** Evaluate the performance of security personnel in controlling access and responding to incidents.
- **Security Policies and Procedures:** Review the effectiveness of security policies and procedures implemented by the security team.

5. Access Control:

- **Biometric Systems**: Assess the reliability and accuracy of biometric access control systems.
- **Keycard and Badge Systems:** Evaluate the security of keycard and badge access systems.

6. Intrusion Detection:

- **Physical Intrusion Detection Systems:** Check the effectiveness of systems that detect physical intrusions, such as motion sensors.

7. Physical Red Teaming:

- **Simulated Attacks**: Conduct simulated physical attacks to test the response of security personnel and the effectiveness of security measures.

8. Social Engineering:

- **Tailgating**: Test the susceptibility of employees to tailgating attempts, where an unauthorized person follows an authorized person into a secured area.

- **Impersonation**: Evaluate the effectiveness of security personnel in verifying the identity of individuals.

9. Emergency Response:

- **Evacuation Procedures**: Assess the organization's emergency response and evacuation procedures.

- **Emergency Exits:** Ensure that emergency exits are clearly marked and easily accessible.

10. Documentation and Reporting:

- **Documentation:** Provide a detailed report of findings, including vulnerabilities identified and recommendations for improvement.

- **Risk Assessment**: Assess the level of risk associated with identified vulnerabilities.

Blended attacks:

In the context of cybersecurity and penetration testing, a blended assault is a complex and multidimensional strategy in which an attacker mixes numerous approaches and strategies to exploit weaknesses and achieve their objectives. The word "blended" refers to the combination of various assault vectors or techniques to defeat defences and improve the chance of success.

Here are the key elements and characteristics of blended attacks:

1. **Diverse Attack Vectors:**
   - Blended attacks may involve a combination of different attack vectors, such as social engineering, network exploits, and physical intrusion. This diversity makes it challenging for defenders to anticipate and mitigate all aspects of the attack.

2. **Social Engineering Component:**
   - Social engineering plays a significant role in blended attacks. Attackers may use tactics to manipulate individuals within the target organization, such as phishing emails, impersonation, or phone calls, to gain access to sensitive information or systems.

3. Exploitation of Multiple Weaknesses:

- Blended attacks often exploit multiple weaknesses across various layers of an organization's security infrastructure. This could include exploiting vulnerabilities in network systems, applications, and human factors.

4. Coordinated Timing:

- The different components of a blended attack are often coordinated in terms of timing. For example, a social engineering attack may precede or coincide with a network penetration attempt, creating confusion and diverting attention.

5. Adaptability:

- Blended attacks are adaptive and can adjust their tactics based on the evolving security landscape. Attackers may change their strategies in response to the target organization's countermeasures or defensive measures.

6. Focus on Weakest Links:

- Blended attacks often target the weakest links in the security chain, whether it's exploiting a known software vulnerability, manipulating a human operator, or finding a gap in physical security.

7. Increased Complexity:

- These attacks are generally more complex compared to single-vector attacks. The combination of different methods requires a higher level of planning, sophistication, and technical expertise.

8. **Harder to Detect:**

- The multifaceted nature of blended attacks makes them more challenging to detect using traditional security measures. Security teams need to be vigilant and employ a variety of detection mechanisms to identify and respond to such attacks.

9. **Goal-Oriented:**

- Blended attacks are goal-oriented, aiming to achieve specific objectives, such as gaining unauthorized access, exfiltrating sensitive data, or causing disruption. The combination of tactics is chosen strategically to increase the likelihood of success in reaching these goals.

Chapter 9: Web Application Penetration Testing

Web application security principles:

Online application security is an important part of cybersecurity that entails putting in place safeguards to protect online applications from various threats and vulnerabilities. Here are some fundamental web application security ideas and concepts:

1. **Input Validation:**

   - Ensure that all user inputs, whether from forms, URLs, or any other sources, are validated before processing.

   - Use input validation mechanisms to check for malicious input, such as SQL injection, cross-site scripting (XSS), and other injection attacks.

2. **Authentication and Authorization:**

   - Implement secure authentication mechanisms to verify the identity of users.

   - Enforce proper authorization to control access to different parts of the web application based on user roles and permissions.

3. **Session Management:**

   - Use secure session management techniques to protect user sessions.

   - Employ secure session tokens, and consider implementing features like session timeouts and token regeneration.

4. **Secure Communication:**

   - Use HTTPS (SSL/TLS) to encrypt data transmitted between the client and the server.

   - Protect against man-in-the-middle attacks by ensuring secure communication channels.

5. **Cross-Site Scripting (XSS) Protection:**

   - Validate and sanitize user inputs to prevent the injection of malicious scripts into web pages.

   - Implement content security policies (CSP) to mitigate the impact of XSS attacks.

6. **Cross-Site Request Forgery (CSRF) Protection:**

   - Use anti-CSRF tokens to verify that requests made to the server are legitimate and not forged by malicious actors.

7. **Security Headers:**

   - Implement security headers in HTTP responses to enhance the overall security posture of the web application.

   - Examples include Strict-Transport-Security, Content-Security-Policy, and X-Frame-Options headers.

8. File Upload Security:

- If the application allows file uploads, validate file types and implement proper file upload restrictions.

- Ensure that uploaded files cannot be executed as scripts or used to exploit other vulnerabilities.

9. Error Handling and Logging:

- Provide custom error messages to users without revealing sensitive information.

- Implement proper logging mechanisms to monitor and analyze security events.

10. Database Security:

- Use parameterized queries and prepared statements to prevent SQL injection attacks.

- Implement the principle of least privilege for database access.

11. Security Patching and Updates:

- Regularly update and patch both the web application and its dependencies to address known vulnerabilities.

- Monitor security advisories for the technologies used in the application.

12. Security Testing:

- Conduct regular security assessments, including penetration testing and code reviews.

- Use automated tools to scan for common vulnerabilities, but also perform manual testing for more complex issues.

13. **Client-Side Security:**

- Validate and sanitize data on the client side to reduce the risk of manipulation.

- Be cautious about relying solely on client-side security measures, as they can be bypassed.

14. **Security Education and Awareness:**

- Train developers, administrators, and users on security best practices.

- Foster a security-aware culture to reduce the risk of social engineering attacks.

SQL injection:

SQL injection is a sort of cyber attack in which an attacker manipulates an application's SQL query by inserting malicious SQL code into input fields. When user input is directly integrated into SQL queries without sufficient validation or sanitization, this vulnerability occurs. SQL injection has major effects since it allows attackers to overcome authentication, obtain, alter, or remove data, and even perform administrative activities on a database.

A more extensive description of SQL injection may be found here:

1. Vulnerability Point: User Input

- SQL injection exploits applications that use user input in constructing SQL queries without properly validating or sanitizing the input.

2. Types of SQL Injection:

- **Classic SQL Injection**: Involves manipulating a query by injecting malicious SQL code.

- **Blind SQL Injection:** The attacker doesn't directly see the results of the injected code but can infer information based on the application's response.

3. How SQL Injection Works:

- **User Input in SQL Query**: Applications often take user input to construct SQL queries dynamically. For example, a login form might construct a query like: `SELECT * FROM users WHERE username = 'input_username' AND password = 'input_password';`

- **Malicious Input**: An attacker can manipulate the input field by providing something like `` '' OR '1'='1'; —``. When injected, the query becomes: `SELECT * FROM users WHERE username = '' OR '1'='1'; —' AND password = 'input_password';`

- **Result:** This modification results in a query that always returns true for the password check, effectively bypassing the login mechanism.

4. Common SQL Injection Techniques:

- **Union-Based SQL Injection:** Injects a UNION statement to combine results from another table.

- **Time-Based Blind SQL Injection:** Delays the server's response to reveal information.

- **Error-Based SQL Injection:** Exploits error messages to gather information about the database structure.

5. Prevention and Mitigation:

- **Input Validation:** Validate and sanitize user input. Use parameterized queries or prepared statements to ensure separation between data and SQL code.

- **Least Privilege Principle:** Restrict database user privileges. Avoid using accounts with unnecessary permissions.

- **Web Application Firewalls (WAF):** Employ WAFs to detect and block malicious SQL injection attempts.

- **Regular Security Audits:** Regularly audit code and conduct security assessments to identify and fix vulnerabilities.

6. Examples of Impact:

- **Unauthorized Access:** Attackers can bypass authentication and gain unauthorized access to a system.

- **Data Manipulation:** Attackers can read, modify, or delete data within a database.

- **Database Takeover**: In extreme cases, attackers might gain control of the entire database server.

Cross-site scripting (XSS) and other web vulnerabilities:

Cross-site scripting (XSS) is a sort of security flaw that arises when an attacker injects malicious scripts onto web pages that other users are viewing. When launched by a victim's browser, these scripts can do a variety of malicious operations, including stealing user data, session tokens, or even defacing websites. XSS flaws are ubiquitous in online applications and can have major security consequences.

Cross-site scripting (XSS) and other web vulnerabilities are explained here:

1. **Cross-Site Scripting (XSS):**
   - **Reflected XSS:** The injected script is embedded in a URL or other input and is reflected to the user by the web application. The attacker usually tricks the victim into clicking a malicious link containing the payload.

- **Stored XSS:** The injected script is permanently stored on the target server, often in a database. When a user accesses a specific page, the script is served to their browser.

2. Cross-Site Request Forgery (CSRF):

- CSRF occurs when an attacker tricks a user's browser into making an unintended request. This can lead to actions being performed on behalf of the victim without their consent. It often involves manipulating the victim's session, leading to unauthorized transactions or changes in the application's state.

3. SQL Injection:

- SQL injection involves injecting malicious SQL queries into input fields. If the web application does not properly validate or sanitize user inputs, an attacker can manipulate the SQL queries, potentially gaining unauthorized access to the database or executing other malicious actions.

4. Security Misconfigurations:

- Security misconfigurations occur when a web application is not securely configured. This can include default credentials, unnecessary services or features enabled, or improper access controls. Attackers can exploit these misconfigurations to gain unauthorized access or perform other malicious activities.

5. Cross-Origin Resource Sharing (CORS) Issues:

- CORS is a security feature implemented by web browsers to control how web pages in one domain can request and interact with resources in another domain. Misconfigurations in CORS policies can lead to unauthorized cross-origin requests, potentially exposing sensitive information.

6. File Upload Vulnerabilities:

- Insecure file upload mechanisms can allow an attacker to upload malicious files, leading to various security risks. This could include executing arbitrary code, escalating privileges, or compromising the integrity of the web application.

7. Security Headers:

- Missing or misconfigured security headers, such as Content Security Policy (CSP), can expose web applications to various attacks. Security headers help protect against XSS, clickjacking, and other web-based attacks by controlling how browsers handle content.

8. XML External Entity (XXE) Injection:

- XXE occurs when an attacker can influence the processing of XML data, leading to the disclosure of internal files, denial of service, or other security issues.

Chapter 10: Mobile Application Penetration Testing

Mobile security challenges:

Because of the growing usage of smartphones and tablets, as well as the rising complexity of mobile ecosystems, mobile security confronts various problems. Here are some of the most pressing issues in mobile security:

1. **Device Diversity:**
   - The vast array of mobile devices running different operating systems (iOS, Android, etc.) and versions makes it challenging to create security measures that apply universally.

2. **Operating System Fragmentation:**
   - Android, in particular, suffers from fragmentation, with many devices running older versions of the operating system that may lack the latest security updates and features.

3. App Stores and Malware:

- App stores are popular targets for malware distribution. Malicious apps can be disguised as legitimate ones, and users may inadvertently download and install them, leading to potential security breaches.

4. Data Protection:

- Mobile devices often store sensitive personal and business data. Ensuring the confidentiality and integrity of this data is a challenge, especially if the device is lost or stolen.

5. Insecure Applications:

- Vulnerabilities in mobile applications can expose devices to various security risks. Developers may inadvertently introduce flaws, and users may not always update apps promptly, leaving their devices susceptible to exploitation.

6. Network Security:

- Mobile devices frequently connect to various networks, including public Wi-Fi. This exposes them to potential man-in-the-middle attacks, eavesdropping, and other network-based security threats.

7. BYOD (Bring Your Device) Policies:

- The trend of employees using personal devices for work purposes introduces security challenges. Striking a balance between user convenience and enforcing security measures is crucial.

8. Jailbreaking and Rooting:

- Users might intentionally remove restrictions on their devices through processes like jailbreaking (iOS) or rooting (Android), which can undermine built-in security features and expose the device to additional risks.

9. Biometric Security Concerns:

- Biometric authentication methods (fingerprint, facial recognition) are becoming more common, but they are not without vulnerabilities. Storing and securing biometric data is a critical challenge.

10. Lack of User Awareness:

- Users might not be fully aware of the potential security risks associated with mobile devices. This lack of awareness can lead to unsafe practices, such as downloading apps from untrusted sources.

11. Phishing Attacks:

- Mobile devices are susceptible to phishing attacks through emails, text messages, or malicious websites. Users may unknowingly disclose sensitive information, compromising the security of their devices.

12. Limited Security Controls:

- Mobile platforms may have limitations on the level of security controls that users and administrators can implement, making it challenging to enforce robust security policies.

Android and iOS vulnerabilities:

The two leading mobile operating systems, Android and iOS, are vulnerable to a variety of vulnerabilities that attackers might exploit. Here is a rundown of the most prevalent vulnerabilities linked with each platform:

Android Vulnerabilities:

1. **Fragmentation**:
   - Android devices come from various manufacturers and carriers, leading to fragmentation in terms of software versions and security patches. Some devices may not receive timely updates, leaving them vulnerable.

2. **Malicious Apps:**
   - The open nature of the Android ecosystem allows the installation of apps from third-party sources. Users may inadvertently download malicious apps that can compromise the device.

3. **Privilege Escalation:**

- Vulnerabilities in the Android operating system may allow attackers to escalate their privileges, gaining unauthorized access to sensitive information or control over the device.

4. **Side-loading of Apps:**

- Android allows users to install apps from sources other than the official Google Play Store. If users download apps from untrusted sources, they might expose themselves to security risks.

5. **Man-in-the-Middle Attacks:**

- Android devices can be susceptible to man-in-the-middle attacks, especially when connected to unsecured Wi-Fi networks. This can lead to the interception of sensitive data.

6. **Outdated Software:**

- Users may not update their devices regularly, leading to exposure to known vulnerabilities that have been patched in later versions of the operating system.

iOS Vulnerabilities:

1. **Jailbreaking:**

- Jailbreaking an iOS device removes Apple's restrictions on app installation and allows users to install unauthorized apps. While this offers greater customization, it also opens up the device to potential security risks.

2. Malicious Apps:

- Although the App Store is curated, malicious apps can occasionally bypass Apple's review process. Users who jailbreak their devices and install apps from unofficial sources are particularly at risk.

3. iMessage and SMS Vulnerabilities:

- Vulnerabilities in iMessage or the handling of SMS messages can be exploited for attacks, including phishing attempts and the delivery of malicious payloads.

4. WiFi and Bluetooth Attacks:

- iOS devices may be vulnerable to attacks when connected to insecure Wi-Fi networks or through Bluetooth vulnerabilities. This can potentially lead to unauthorized access or data interception.

5. WebKit Exploits:

- The WebKit engine powers the Safari browser on iOS. Exploits targeting WebKit vulnerabilities can lead to arbitrary code execution, enabling attackers to compromise the device.

6. Zero-Day Exploits:

- Like any sophisticated operating system, iOS is not immune to zero-day vulnerabilities. These are unknown vulnerabilities that can be exploited by attackers before a patch is available.

Mobile application testing tools:

Mobile application testing is an important part of the software development lifecycle since it ensures that mobile apps work as intended and fulfil quality requirements. There are several tools available to help with mobile application testing, and these tools address various areas of the testing process. Here are a few examples of regularly used mobile application testing tools:

1. **Appium:**

   - **Type:** Open-source

   - **Purpose**: Appium is a widely used automation tool for testing mobile applications on Android and iOS platforms. It supports multiple programming languages and allows for cross-platform testing.

2. **XCTest and XCUITest:**

   - **Type:** Native iOS testing tools

   - **Purpose**: XCTest is the testing framework for Swift and Objective-C applications, and XCUITest is Apple's UI testing framework for iOS apps. These tools are integrated into Xcode, Apple's official development environment.

3. **Espresso:**

   - **Type:** Native Android testing tool

- **Purpose**: Espresso is the UI testing framework for Android applications. It is part of the Android Testing Support Library and provides a rich set of APIs for creating UI tests.

4. Calabash:

- **Type:** Open-source

- **Purpose**: Calabash is an open-source mobile application testing framework that supports both Android and iOS. It allows for the creation of cross-platform tests using Cucumber, a behaviour-driven development (BDD) tool.

5. Selendroid:

- **Type:** Open-source

- **Purpose**: Selendroid is a test automation framework for Android apps. It is compatible with the Selenium WebDriver API and supports testing of native, hybrid, and mobile web applications.

6. Detox:

- **Type:** Open-source

- **Purpose**: Detox is a grey-box end-to-end testing library for React Native applications. It focuses on the automation of interaction with the app and helps in simulating real user interactions.

7. Robot Framework with Appium Library:

- **Type:** Open-source

- **Purpose:** Robot Framework is a generic test automation framework that can be extended with various libraries. The Appium

Library allows Robot Framework to interact with mobile applications using Appium.

8. TestComplete Mobile:

- **Type:** Commercial

- **Purpose**: TestComplete is a commercial testing tool that supports mobile application testing on both Android and iOS platforms. It provides a variety of testing capabilities, including recording and playback, scripting, and object recognition.

9. Katalon Studio:

- **Type**: Free and commercial versions available

- **Purpose**: Katalon Studio is an all-in-one test automation solution that supports mobile testing along with web and API testing. It is user-friendly and suitable for both beginners and experienced testers.

10. Firebase Test Lab:

- **Type:** Cloud-based

- **Purpose**: Firebase Test Lab is a cloud-based testing infrastructure provided by Google. It allows you to test your app on a wide range of devices in the cloud, providing valuable insights into the app's performance and compatibility.

Consider platform support, convenience of use, integration capabilities, and the unique testing demands of your mobile app when selecting a mobile application testing solution. The correct tool

is chosen based on the project needs and the development team's
testing   strategy.

Chapter 11: Cloud Security Testing

Cloud computing risks and challenges:

Cloud computing has many advantages, such as flexibility, scalability, and cost-effectiveness, but it also has its own set of hazards and concerns. The following are some of the most prevalent dangers and obstacles related to cloud computing:

1. **Security Concerns:**
   - **Data Breaches**: Storing sensitive data in the cloud raises concerns about unauthorized access and data breaches.
   - **Identity and Access Management (IAM):** Improperly configured IAM settings can lead to unauthorized access to resources.
   - **Insecure Interfaces and APIs**: Weaknesses in the interfaces and APIs used to access cloud services can be exploited by attackers.

2. **Compliance and Legal Issues:**
   - **Data Jurisdiction:** Different countries have different regulations regarding data storage and privacy. Cloud users must ensure compliance with relevant laws.

- **Auditing and Reporting:** Meeting compliance standards and providing audit trails can be challenging in a shared cloud environment.

3. Data Loss:

- **Data Deletion**: Accidental or intentional data deletion can result in the permanent loss of important information.

- **Service Provider Reliability:** Dependence on a third-party service provider makes data vulnerable to provider outages or shutdowns.

4. Lack of Control:

- **Limited Customization:** Users may have limited control over the underlying infrastructure and configurations in a public cloud environment.

- **Dependency on Service Providers**: Organizations rely on the security measures implemented by cloud service providers.

5. Limited Visibility and Transparency:

- **Monitoring Challenges:** Limited visibility into the provider's infrastructure can make it challenging to monitor and detect security incidents.

- **Transparency:** Some cloud service providers may not disclose detailed information about their security practices, making it difficult for users to assess risks.

6. Network Security:

- **Shared Resources:** Multi-tenancy introduces the risk that malicious activity in one part of the cloud could impact the security and performance of other users.

- **Interception of Data in Transit:** Data transmitted between the user and the cloud provider may be intercepted if not properly secured.

7. Downtime and Service Availability:

- **Service Outages:** Cloud services can experience downtime due to technical issues or cyber-attacks, affecting the availability of applications and data.

- **Dependency on Internet Connectivity:** Reliance on Internet connectivity means that disruptions in connectivity can impact access to cloud resources.

8. Vendor Lock-in:

- **Dependency on a Single Provider**: Transitioning from one cloud service provider to another can be complex, leading to vendor lock-in and potential difficulties in migrating data and applications.

9. Insider Threats:

- **Unauthorized Access:** Insiders, including employees of the cloud service provider, may pose a threat if they gain unauthorized access to sensitive information.

10. **Inadequate Due Diligence:**

   - **Failure to Assess Risks:** Organizations may not conduct thorough risk assessments before migrating to the cloud, leading to inadequate security measures.

Testing cloud infrastructure and services:

Testing cloud infrastructure and services is an important part of cloud computing penetration testing. Cloud infrastructures, such as Amazon Web Services (AWS), Microsoft Azure, or Google Cloud Platform, provide distinct problems and security concerns. Here's an explanation of cloud infrastructure and service testing:

1. **Understanding Cloud Infrastructure:**

   - **Virtualization and Shared Resources:** Cloud services often rely on virtualization, where multiple virtual machines share the same physical hardware. Penetration testers need to understand how virtualization works and identify potential security risks.

2. **Cloud Configuration Security:**

   - **Security Group and Firewall Rules:** Testing the configuration of security groups and firewall rules is essential. Misconfigurations can lead to unauthorized access or exposure to sensitive services.

3. Identity and Access Management (IAM) Testing:

- **User Permissions and Roles:** Assessing the IAM setup to ensure that users have the least privilege necessary is crucial. Penetration testers need to identify and exploit misconfigurations related to user roles and permissions.

4. Data Security:

- **Data Encryption:** Evaluating how data is encrypted in transit and at rest is vital. This includes assessing the use of secure communication protocols and the effectiveness of encryption mechanisms for stored data.

5. Network Security:

- **Virtual Private Cloud (VPC) Security:** Testing the security of the VPC, including network segmentation, subnets, and routing configurations, is essential to prevent unauthorized lateral movement within the cloud environment.

6. Application Security:

- **Web Application Security:** If there are web applications hosted in the cloud, penetration testers should assess them for common vulnerabilities such as injection attacks, cross-site scripting (XSS), and other web-related security issues.

7. Container Security:

- **Docker and Kubernetes Security:** Assessing the security of containerized environments is crucial. This includes evaluating

Docker configurations, Kubernetes orchestrations, and the security of container images.

8. Serverless Security:

- **Function as a Service (FaaS):** For serverless architectures, penetration testers need to assess the security of serverless functions, including function permissions, input validation, and potential vulnerabilities.

9. Monitoring and Logging:

- **CloudTrail and Logging Services:** Analyzing cloud provider logs and monitoring configurations is essential for detecting and responding to security incidents. Penetration testers may attempt to manipulate logs or evade detection mechanisms.

10. Incident Response Testing:

- **Cloud Incident Response Plan:** Evaluating the effectiveness of the cloud incident response plan is crucial. This includes assessing how well the organization can detect and respond to security incidents in the cloud environment.

11. Compliance and Governance:

- **Regulatory Compliance**: Ensuring that the cloud environment complies with relevant regulations and industry standards is vital. Penetration testers may assess the implementation of security controls and policies.

12. **Data Backups and Recovery:**

- **Backup Security:** Assessing the security of data backups, including the integrity and confidentiality of backup data, is important. This ensures that organizations can recover from data loss or compromise.

13. **External Service Dependencies:**

- **Third-Party Services:** Many cloud environments rely on external services. Penetration testers should assess the security of these dependencies and their potential impact on the overall security of the cloud infrastructure.

Cloud security best practices:

Cloud security is becoming increasingly important in information technology as more firms move their data and apps to the cloud. The following are some excellent practices for improving cloud security:

1. **Data Encryption:**

- **In-Transit Encryption:** Encrypt data when it's being transmitted between your organization and the cloud service provider. This is typically achieved using protocols such as TLS/SSL.

- **At-Rest Encryption:** Ensure that data stored in the cloud is encrypted. Many cloud providers offer encryption services or allow customers to use their encryption keys.

2. Access Control:

- **Identity and Access Management (IAM):** Implement strong identity management and access controls. Use role-based access control (RBAC) to assign permissions based on job responsibilities.

- **Multi-Factor Authentication (MFA):** Enforce the use of multi-factor authentication for accessing cloud services, adding an extra layer of security beyond just passwords.

3. Regular Audits and Monitoring:

- **Audit Logs:** Regularly review and analyze audit logs provided by the cloud service provider to detect any unusual activities.

- **Continuous Monitoring**: Implement continuous monitoring to identify and respond to security incidents in real-time.

4. Secure APIs:

- **API Security**: If your organization uses APIs to connect with cloud services, ensure that they are secured. This includes using authentication mechanisms, encryption, and proper access controls.

5. Data Backups and Disaster Recovery:

- **Regular Backups:** Ensure regular backups of critical data stored in the cloud, and test the restoration process periodically.

- **Disaster Recovery Plan:** Develop and implement a comprehensive disaster recovery plan to minimize downtime in case of a security incident.

6. Security Patching:

- **Stay Updated:** Keep all software and systems, including the underlying infrastructure provided by the cloud service, up to date with the latest security patches.

7. Network Security:

- **Virtual Private Cloud (VPC):** Utilize VPCs or similar network isolation mechanisms to control and secure the flow of data between different components of your cloud infrastructure.

- **Firewalls and Security Groups:** Implement firewalls and security groups to restrict unauthorized access to cloud resources.

8. Incident Response Planning:

- **Response Plan:** Have a well-defined incident response plan in place. This includes procedures for identifying, containing, eradicating, recovering, and learning from security incidents.

9. Data Governance:

- **Data Classification**: Classify data based on its sensitivity, and apply appropriate security controls accordingly.

- **Data Retention Policies**: Establish and enforce data retention policies to ensure unnecessary data is not stored in the cloud.

10. **Compliance:**

- **Understand Regulatory Requirements:** Be aware of and comply with industry-specific and regional regulations governing data protection and privacy.

11. **Employee Training:**

- **Security Awareness:** Provide regular training for employees on security best practices, especially focusing on the unique challenges and considerations of cloud environments.

12. **Collaboration with Cloud Service Provider:**

- **Understand Shared Responsibility**: Clearly understand the shared responsibility model with the cloud service provider. Know which security aspects are the responsibility of the provider and which are the responsibility of the customer.

Implementing these recommended practices may greatly improve an organization's cloud infrastructure's security posture. It's critical to keep current on the threat landscape and adapt security measures accordingly.

Chapter 12: Incident Response and Reporting

Developing an incident response plan:

Creating an incident response plan is a vital component of any company's cybersecurity strategy. An incident response plan lays out the processes and activities to be done in the case of a cybersecurity incident, to limit damage, shorten recovery time, and preserve evidence for investigation. Here's a more extensive breakdown of the essential elements needed in creating an incident response plan:

1. Preparation:

- **Identifying Assets:** Determine the critical assets and data that need protection. This includes both physical and digital assets.

- **Risk Assessment:** Evaluate potential risks and threats to the organization. This analysis helps prioritize resources and efforts in incident response planning.

2. Formation of an Incident Response Team (IRT):

- **Roles and Responsibilities:** Define the roles and responsibilities of individuals within the incident response team. This may include a team lead, investigators, communicators, legal advisors, and IT personnel.

- **Training and Drills:** Ensure that team members are adequately trained and conduct regular drills to test the efficiency and effectiveness of the incident response plan.

3. Incident Identification and Classification:

- **Detection Systems:** Implement and maintain systems that can detect potential security incidents. This may include intrusion detection systems, security information and event management (SIEM) tools, and antivirus solutions.

- **Incident Classification**: Develop criteria for classifying incidents based on severity and impact. This helps prioritize the response efforts.

4. Incident Containment:

- **Isolation Procedures:** Define procedures for isolating affected systems to prevent further damage and limit the scope of the incident.

- **Communication Protocols:** Establish communication channels for the incident response team to coordinate containment efforts.

5. Eradication and Recovery:

- **Root Cause Analysis:** Conduct a thorough analysis to determine the root cause of the incident. This information is crucial for preventing similar incidents in the future.

- **System Restoration**: Develop procedures for restoring affected systems to normal operation while ensuring that the security vulnerabilities are addressed.

6. Communication and Reporting:

- **Internal Communication:** communication channels within the organization for updating key stakeholders, including management, employees, and the incident response team.

- **External Communication:** Establish protocols for communicating with external parties, such as law enforcement, regulatory bodies, and affected customers.

7. Documentation:

- **Incident Logs**: Maintain detailed logs of the incident response process, including actions taken, communications, and outcomes.

- **Post-Incident Analysis:** Conduct a post-incident analysis to identify areas for improvement in the incident response plan.

8. Legal and Compliance Considerations:

- **Legal Advisors:** Involve legal counsel to guide compliance with applicable laws and regulations.

- **Evidence Preservation:** Develop procedures for preserving digital evidence to support potential legal actions or investigations.

9. **Continuous Improvement:**

- **Feedback Loops:** Establish mechanisms for collecting feedback from each incident response to continually refine and improve the incident response plan.

- **Updates and Revisions:** Regularly update the incident response plan to incorporate lessons learned, changes in technology, and evolving threat landscapes.

10. **Public Relations:**

- **Media Handling**: Develop strategies for managing public relations during and after a cybersecurity incident, ensuring that the organization's reputation is protected.

Reporting findings and recommendations:

An important element of the penetration testing process is reporting results and suggestions. The report's objective is to convey the penetration test results to stakeholders such as management, system administrators, and other relevant parties. This phase is explained in further depth below:

1. **Documentation of Findings:**

- **Vulnerabilities:** Document each identified vulnerability, including a description of the issue, its severity, and the affected systems or applications.

- **Exploited Weaknesses**: If any systems were successfully exploited during the test, provide details on how the exploitation occurred and the potential impact.

2. **Risk Assessment:**

- **Risk Severity**: Assign a severity level to each identified vulnerability based on the potential impact on the organization.

- **Risk Likelihood**: Assess the likelihood of each vulnerability being exploited, taking into account factors such as ease of exploitation and existing mitigations.

3. **Executive Summary:**

- Provide a high-level overview of the key findings and their implications for the organization.

- Summarize the overall security posture and any significant risks that need immediate attention.

4. **Technical Details:**

- Offer in-depth technical details for each vulnerability, including proof-of-concept code, screenshots, and any additional supporting evidence.

- Include information on the tools and methodologies used during the penetration test.

5. Recommendations:

- **Mitigation Strategies:** Propose specific actions and strategies to address each identified vulnerability. This may involve patching systems, reconfiguring settings, or implementing additional security controls.

- **Priority Ranking:** Prioritize recommendations based on the severity and potential impact of each vulnerability.

- **Long-Term Security Improvements**: Suggest overarching security improvements that can enhance the organization's overall security posture.

6. Non-Technical Recommendations:

- Provide recommendations for non-technical aspects, such as employee training, security policies, and incident response procedures.

- Address any weaknesses in the organization's security culture or awareness.

7. Compliance and Best Practices:

- Assess the organization's compliance with relevant industry standards and regulations.

- Provide recommendations to align the organization with best cybersecurity practices.

8. Reporting Format:

- Present the findings and recommendations in a clear and organized format that is accessible to both technical and non-technical stakeholders.

- Include visuals such as graphs or charts to illustrate the distribution of vulnerabilities and their severity.

9. **Follow-Up Actions:**
    - Specify any follow-up actions required from the organization, such as regular security assessments, training programs, or further investigation into specific issues.

10. **Legal and Ethical Considerations:**
    - Clearly state the boundaries of the penetration test to avoid any misunderstandings or legal implications.
    - Emphasize the ethical nature of the testing and the intention to improve security rather than cause harm.

Post-testing cleanup and documentation:

Post-testing cleaning and documentation are essential components of the penetration testing process. Following the completion of the penetration testing operations, it is critical to verify that the environment is restored to its original form and that adequate documentation is delivered to the customer. Here's a more extensive breakdown of these elements:

1. **Cleanup:**

   - **Reversing Changes:** During the testing process, the penetration tester might make changes to the system or network to demonstrate vulnerabilities or exploits. It's crucial to reverse these changes to avoid any unintended or potentially harmful modifications. This might include removing backdoors, deleting test files, or undoing configuration changes.

- **Restoring Configurations:** If configurations were altered for testing purposes, such as firewall rules or user privileges, these configurations need to be restored to their original state. This ensures that the system or network is returned to its normal and secure operational state.

- **Patching Vulnerabilities:** In some cases, the penetration tester may identify and exploit vulnerabilities that were not known to the client. It's common practice to provide recommendations for patching or mitigating these vulnerabilities to improve overall security.

- **Clean Log Files:** During testing, log files may capture activities related to the penetration testing. Cleaning up these log files ensures that sensitive information is not left behind and that the logs accurately reflect the system's normal operation.

2. **Documentation:**

   - **Executive Summary:** A high-level summary of the testing process and key findings. This is often written for non-technical stakeholders and provides an overview of the security posture of the system or network.

- **Detailed Report**: A more in-depth document that includes detailed information about the vulnerabilities identified, the methods used to exploit them, and the potential impact on the system. This is typically intended for technical staff responsible for remediation.

- **Risk Assessment:** An analysis of the risks associated with the identified vulnerabilities. This may include a prioritized list of vulnerabilities based on their severity and potential impact on the organization.

- **Remediation Recommendations:** Specific recommendations for addressing and mitigating the identified vulnerabilities. This could include applying patches, updating configurations, or implementing additional security measures.

- **Evidence of Exploitation:** If the penetration tester was able to successfully exploit vulnerabilities, evidence and details of the exploitation may be included in the documentation. This helps the client understand the potential impact and verify the validity of the findings.

- **Lessons Learned:** Recommendations for improving security practices based on the findings of the penetration test. This can include suggestions for enhancing policies, procedures, and employee training.

- **Legal and Compliance Considerations**: Documentation may also include information related to legal and compliance considerations, especially if the testing involved activities that could have legal implications.

The purpose of post-testing cleaning and documentation is to ensure that the client has a clear knowledge of their systems' security posture, detected vulnerabilities, and activities they can take to improve their security. It also aids in the preservation of openness, accountability, and adherence to ethical norms in the field of penetration   testing.

Chapter 13: Advanced Persistent Threats (APTs)

Understanding APTs:

Definition of APTs:

- An Advanced Persistent Threat (APT) is a sophisticated, long-term cyberattack where an unauthorized user gains access to a network and remains undetected for an extended period.

- APTs are often state-sponsored or carried out by well-funded, organized cybercriminal groups.

Characteristics of APTs:

- **Persistence**: APTs aim to maintain a presence within a target network for an extended duration, allowing attackers to gather valuable information over time.

- **Sophistication:** APTs often involve advanced techniques, including zero-day exploits, customized malware, and social engineering, making them difficult to detect.

- **Targeted**: APTs are typically directed towards specific organizations, industries, or even individuals, to steal sensitive data or disrupt operations.

Lifecycle of APTs:

- **Reconnaissance**: Attackers conduct thorough research to understand the target's infrastructure, employees, and security measures.

- **Initial Compromise**: APTs usually begin with a targeted attack, often exploiting vulnerabilities through spear-phishing emails or other social engineering tactics.

- **Establish Foothold:** Once inside the network, attackers work to establish a persistent presence, often using backdoors or other covert methods.

- **Escalate Privileges**: APTs seek to gain higher levels of access, compromising privileged accounts to navigate freely within the network.

- **Internal Reconnaissance**: Attackers explore the internal network, identifying valuable assets and planning their next moves.

- **Data Exfiltration:** APTs aim to steal sensitive data gradually, often maintaining a low profile to avoid detection.

- **Maintain Presence:** The attackers continue to exploit the compromised system, adapting to security measures and evolving their tactics.

Detection and Prevention:

- **Anomaly Detection**: APTs can be challenging to detect using traditional security measures. Implementing anomaly detection systems that identify unusual patterns of behaviour is crucial.
    - **Endpoint Protection**: Robust endpoint security solutions help prevent initial compromises and detect malicious activities on individual devices.
    - **User Education**: APTs often exploit human vulnerabilities through social engineering. Educating users about phishing, malicious attachments, and other tactics is essential.

Mitigation Strategies:

- Implementing a multi-layered security approach, including firewalls, intrusion detection systems, and regular security audits.
    - Regularly updating and patching software to address vulnerabilities.
    - Developing an incident response plan to minimize damage in case of a successful APT attack.

Detecting and responding to APTs:

Detecting and reacting to Advanced Persistent Threats (APTs) is an important part of cybersecurity because APTs are a sophisticated and persistent type of cyber assault that is frequently carried out by well-funded and coordinated threat actors. APTs are distinguished by their stealthy and targeted nature, to acquire illegal network access and keep that access for a lengthy period. The following are critical components of identifying and responding to APTs:

1. **Threat Intelligence:**

- **Collection and Analysis**: Regularly gather and analyze threat intelligence to understand the tactics, techniques, and procedures (TTPs) employed by APT groups.

- **Indicators of Compromise (IoCs):** Identify and track IoCs, such as malicious IP addresses, domain names, file hashes, and patterns of behaviour associated with APTs.

2. **Anomaly Detection:**

- **Behavioral Analysis**: Implement tools and techniques that monitor normal network behaviour and detect anomalies that may indicate a potential APT.

- **User Behavior Analytics (UBA)**: Analyze user activities to identify abnormal patterns or actions that could be indicative of compromise.

3. **Endpoint Security:**

- **Endpoint Detection and Response (EDR):** Employ EDR solutions to continuously monitor and respond to suspicious activities on endpoints, such as unusual processes or file modifications.

- **Sandboxes and Honeypots:** Use sandboxes and honeypots to analyze and detect malicious code in a controlled environment.

4. Network Monitoring:

- **Intrusion Detection Systems (IDS) and Intrusion Prevention Systems (IPS):** Deploy IDS and IPS to detect and prevent unauthorized access and malicious activities within the network.

- **Packet Capture and Analysis:** Capture and analyze network traffic to identify unusual communication patterns or data exfiltration.

5. Incident Response:

- **Incident Identification:** Establish a robust incident response plan to quickly identify and assess potential APT incidents.

- **Containment and Eradication:** Isolate affected systems, remove malicious components, and remediate vulnerabilities to prevent further compromise.

- **Forensic Analysis:** Conduct thorough forensic analysis to understand the extent of the compromise and gather evidence for future legal or investigative purposes.

6. User Training and Awareness:

- **Phishing Awareness:** Educate users about phishing techniques and social engineering tactics, as APTs often begin with targeted phishing attacks.

- **Security Training**: Provide ongoing security training to employees to enhance their awareness of security threats and best practices.

7. **Continuous Monitoring:**
   - **Security Information and Event Management (SIEM):** Implement SIEM solutions to centralize and analyze security event logs from various sources for real-time monitoring.
   - **Continuous Improvement**: Regularly review and update security measures based on lessons learned from previous incidents and emerging threat intelligence.

8. **Collaboration and Information Sharing:**
   - **Sharing Threat Intelligence:** Participate in threat intelligence sharing communities and share information with other organizations to collectively strengthen defences against APTs.
   - **Collaboration with External Partners:** Work with law enforcement, government agencies, and cybersecurity organizations to report and respond to APT incidents.

9. **Adaptive Security Measures:**
   - **Adaptive Defense:** Implement adaptive security measures that evolve based on the changing threat landscape, ensuring that defences can adapt to new APT tactics and techniques.

APT case studies:

1. Stuxnet:

- **Year:** Discovered in 2010.

- **Target**: Iranian nuclear facilities, particularly those involved in uranium enrichment.

- **Details**: Stuxnet is widely considered one of the most sophisticated cyberweapons ever discovered. It specifically targeted supervisory control and data acquisition (SCADA) systems, affecting programmable logic controllers (PLCs) used in industrial processes. Stuxnet's complexity and precision suggest the involvement of a nation-state.

2. Operation Aurora:

- **Year:** 2009.

- **Target**: Multiple major American corporations, particularly Google.

- **Details**: Believed to be orchestrated by Chinese hackers, Operation Aurora aimed at stealing intellectual property and sensitive information from several large companies. The attackers exploited vulnerabilities in Internet Explorer to gain access to their targets.

3. APT28 (Fancy Bear):

- **Year:** Ongoing, first publicly disclosed in 2014.

- **Targets**: Various governments, military organizations, and political groups.

- **Details**: APT28 is a Russian-sponsored APT group known for its involvement in cyber-espionage activities. It has been linked to various high-profile incidents, including attacks on the Democratic National Committee (DNC) during the 2016 U.S. presidential election.

4. Equifax Data Breach:

- **Year:** 2017.

- Target: Equifax, one of the largest credit reporting agencies.

- **Details**: While not a traditional APT in terms of nation-state involvement, the Equifax breach is considered an advanced and persistent attack. Hackers exploited a vulnerability in Apache Struts to gain unauthorized access to the sensitive personal information of nearly 147 million people.

5. APT29 (Cozy Bear):

- **Year:** Ongoing, first publicly disclosed in 2014.

- **Targets**: Various governments and organizations, including the U.S. government.

- **Details**: APT29 is believed to be a Russian-sponsored group with a history of conducting cyber-espionage campaigns. It gained significant attention for its alleged involvement in the hacking of the Democratic National Committee in 2016.

These case studies demonstrate the wide range of APTs, from critical infrastructure assaults to campaigns targeting political institutions. Advanced tactics, methods, and procedures (TTPs) are frequently used by APTs to retain long-term access and fulfil their objectives without discovery. Remember that the cybersecurity world is always changing, and new APTs and events may have occurred since my previous update.

Chapter 14: Emerging Technologies and Trends

IoT security:

IoT (Internet of Things) security refers to the policies and procedures put in place to safeguard the large network of interconnected devices that comprise the Internet of Things. The Internet of Things (IoT) refers to a wide range of gadgets, including smart household appliances, industrial sensors, medical equipment, and others, all of which are linked to the Internet for data exchange and communication. It is vital to ensure the security of these devices since they frequently handle sensitive information and play a role in key systems.

Here are some important features of IoT security:

1. **Device Security:**

   - **Authentication and Authorization:** Implement strong authentication mechanisms to ensure that only authorized users and devices can access and control IoT devices.

- **Secure Boot and Firmware Updates:** Ensure that IoT devices only boot with authenticated and trusted firmware, and regularly update device firmware to patch vulnerabilities.

2. Communication Security:

- **Encryption:** Use encryption protocols to secure data in transit between IoT devices and the cloud or other endpoints. This prevents unauthorized parties from intercepting and manipulating the data.

- **Secure Protocols**: Employ secure communication protocols such as HTTPS, MQTT, or CoAP, depending on the specific requirements of the IoT application.

3. Network Security:

- **Segmentation**: Segregate IoT devices into separate network segments to minimize the potential for lateral movement by attackers. This helps contain security breaches to a specific subset of devices.

- **Firewalls and Intrusion Detection Systems**: Implement network-level security measures, such as firewalls and intrusion detection systems, to monitor and control traffic to and from IoT devices.

4. Data Security:

- **Data Integrity:** Ensure the integrity of data generated and processed by IoT devices. Unauthorized modifications to data can have serious consequences, especially in critical applications like healthcare or industrial control systems.

- **Data Encryption:** Encrypt stored data on IoT devices to protect it from unauthorized access in case of physical tampering or theft.

5. Device Management and Lifecycle Security:

- **Access Control:** Implement proper access controls to manage permissions for device configuration and management. Only authorized personnel should be able to modify device settings.

- **End-of-Life (EOL) Considerations**: Develop strategies for securely decommissioning and disposing of IoT devices to prevent data leaks or the reuse of compromised hardware.

6. Security Standards and Best Practices:

- **Adherence to Standards**: Follow established security standards and best practices for IoT development and deployment, such as those provided by the Industrial Internet Consortium (IIC) or the Open Web Application Security Project (OWASP).

- **Security Audits and Testing:** Conduct regular security audits and penetration testing to identify and address vulnerabilities in the IoT ecosystem.

7. User Education and Awareness:

- **User Training:** Educate end-users about the security features and best practices associated with IoT devices to reduce the risk of common security pitfalls, such as using weak passwords.

Blockchain security:

Blockchain security is an important part of cybersecurity that focuses on ensuring the integrity, confidentiality, and availability of data and transactions inside a blockchain network. Blockchains are distributed and decentralized ledgers that safeguard and verify transactions using cryptographic techniques. Here are some important characteristics of blockchain security:

1. **Cryptography:**
   - **Hash Functions**: Blockchain uses cryptographic hash functions to secure the integrity of data. Each block in the chain contains a hash of the previous block, creating a chain of blocks.
   - **Digital Signatures:** Digital signatures are used to authenticate the identity of participants and verify the origin of transactions. They ensure that only the authorized parties can modify transactions.

2. **Consensus Mechanisms:**
   - **Proof of Work (PoW) and Proof of Stake (PoS):** These are consensus mechanisms used to validate transactions and secure the network. PoW relies on computational power, while PoS relies on ownership of cryptocurrency.

3. **Smart Contract Security:**
   - **Code Auditing:** Smart contracts, which are self-executing contracts with the terms of the agreement directly written into code,

need to be audited for vulnerabilities. Flaws in smart contracts can lead to significant financial losses.

- **Secure Development Practices:** Developers should follow secure coding practices to minimize the risk of vulnerabilities in smart contracts. This includes avoiding reentrancy attacks, ensuring proper access controls, and thoroughly testing the code.

4. Permissioned vs. Permissionless Blockchains:

- **Access Control:** Permissioned blockchains restrict access to participants, while permissionless blockchains are open to anyone. Access control mechanisms are crucial for maintaining the security and privacy of the network.

5. Network Security:

- **51% Attack:** In a Proof of Work blockchain, a 51% attack occurs when an entity gains control of the majority of the network's mining power, allowing them to control and manipulate the blockchain.

- **Sybil Attack**: In a Sybil attack, an attacker creates multiple fake identities to control a significant portion of the network.

6. Privacy and Anonymity:

- **Zero-Knowledge Proofs**: Techniques like zero-knowledge proofs allow participants to prove possession of certain information without revealing that information. This enhances privacy and anonymity.

- **Confidential Transactions**: Some blockchains implement confidential transactions to hide the transaction amounts, adding an extra layer of privacy.

7. **Regulatory Compliance:**

- **KYC/AML:** Know Your Customer (KYC) and Anti-Money Laundering (AML) regulations may require blockchain participants to verify their identities. Ensuring compliance with these regulations is essential for legal and regulatory acceptance.

8. **Immutable Ledger:**

- **Immutability:** While the immutability of blockchain is a strength, it can pose challenges in cases of errors or fraudulent transactions. Therefore, mechanisms for handling disputes or errors must be considered.

9. **Continuous Monitoring and Incident Response:**

- **Monitoring Tools:** Continuous monitoring of the blockchain network helps detect unusual activities or potential security breaches.

- **Incident Response Plans:** Having plans in place to respond to security incidents is crucial for minimizing damage in case of a breach.

AI and machine learning in cybersecurity:

AI (Artificial Intelligence) and machine learning have evolved into essential components of cybersecurity, providing increased capabilities for detecting, preventing, and responding to cyber-attacks. Here's an outline of how artificial intelligence and machine learning are used in cybersecurity:

1. **Threat Detection and Prevention:**

- **Anomaly Detection:** Machine learning algorithms can establish a baseline of "normal" behaviour within a network or system. Deviations from this baseline can be flagged as potential security threats.

- **Behavioral Analytics:** AI systems can analyze user and system behaviour in real-time to identify unusual patterns that may indicate malicious activities.

2. **Malware Detection:**

- **Signature-based Detection:** Traditional antivirus software uses signature-based detection to identify known malware based on predefined patterns. AI enhances this by continuously updating and improving these signatures.

- **Heuristic-based Detection:** Machine learning models can identify new and previously unseen malware by learning from the behaviour of known threats.

3. Phishing Detection:

- **Natural Language Processing (NLP):** AI can analyze email content using NLP to identify phishing attempts by recognizing suspicious language, requests for sensitive information, or impersonation of legitimate entities.

4. Endpoint Security:

- **Behavioral Analysis:** Machine learning can monitor endpoint activities and detect unusual behaviour indicative of a potential compromise, such as unauthorized access or data exfiltration.

5. Network Security:

- **Intrusion Detection and Prevention Systems (IDPS):** AI-enhanced IDPS can analyze network traffic patterns, detect anomalies, and respond to potential threats in real-time.

- **User and Entity Behavior Analytics (UEBA):** AI tools can identify abnormal user behaviours, helping to prevent insider threats.

6. Incident Response:

- **Automation:** AI can automate routine incident response tasks, allowing cybersecurity teams to focus on more complex and strategic aspects of incident resolution.

- **Threat Intelligence:** Machine learning algorithms can process and analyze vast amounts of threat intelligence data to provide real-time insights into emerging threats.

7. **Authentication and Access Control:**

- **Biometric Authentication:** AI-based biometric systems enhance authentication security by using unique physical or behavioural characteristics for user identification.

- *Adaptive Access Control:* Machine learning can assess user behaviour and adjust access privileges dynamically based on contextual information.

8. **Security Analytics:**

- **Big Data Analysis:** AI and machine learning excel at processing and analyzing large datasets, helping cybersecurity professionals identify trends, correlations, and potential security risks.

9. **Predictive Analysis:**

- **Threat Predictions:** AI models can predict potential cybersecurity threats by analyzing historical data and identifying patterns that may indicate future attacks.

10. **AI in Deception Technologies:**

- **Honeypots and Deception**: AI-driven deception technologies deploy decoy assets to lure attackers, allowing security teams to study and understand the tactics, techniques, and procedures used by adversaries.

Chapter 15: Challenges and Future Directions

Current challenges in penetration testing:

1. Sophisticated Attack Techniques:

- Attackers are constantly improving their approaches, making it difficult for penetration testers to stay up. Advanced evasion strategies, polymorphic malware, and other approaches that can circumvent typical security measures are included.

2. Evolving Technology Landscape:

- The rapid evolution of technology, such as cloud computing, Internet of Things (IoT), and containerization, introduces new attack surfaces and complexities. Penetration testers need to stay current with these technologies and understand their security implications.

3. Complex Network Architectures:

- Organizations often have complex and interconnected network architectures. Testing such environments requires a deep understanding of the systems and potential vulnerabilities, making it time-consuming and challenging.

4. **Compliance and Regulation:**

- Meeting compliance standards and regulations add an extra layer of complexity to penetration testing. Testers need to ensure that their assessments align with industry-specific requirements and legal frameworks.

5. **Lack of Access to Source Code:**

- In black-box testing scenarios where penetration testers don't have access to the source code, identifying vulnerabilities becomes more challenging. Testers must rely solely on external testing methods, such as fuzz testing and reverse engineering.

6. **Human Factors:**

- Social engineering attacks remain a significant threat, and it can be challenging for penetration testers to assess and mitigate the human factor. Phishing, for example, requires a combination of technical and psychological understanding.

7. **False Positives/Negatives**:

- Penetration testing tools may produce false positives or false negatives. Testers need to carefully analyze results to differentiate between real vulnerabilities and erroneous findings. This requires a combination of automated tools and human expertise.

8. **Insufficient Resources:**

- Many organizations may not allocate enough resources, both in terms of time and personnel, for thorough penetration testing. This can result in incomplete assessments that fail to identify all potential vulnerabilities.

9. Vendor Security:

- Organizations increasingly rely on third-party vendors for various services, and these vendors may introduce security risks. Assessing the security posture of external vendors poses a unique challenge for penetration testers.

10. Dynamic Threat Landscape:

- The threat landscape is dynamic, with new vulnerabilities and attack vectors emerging regularly. Penetration testers need to stay informed about the latest threats to ensure their assessments are comprehensive and relevant.

11. Scalability:

- For large organizations or those with a global presence, scaling penetration testing efforts can be a logistical challenge. Coordinating assessments across multiple locations and addressing diverse security concerns requires careful planning.

Future trends and developments in cybersecurity:

1. Artificial Intelligence (AI) and Machine Learning (ML) Integration:

- Increased use of AI and ML for threat detection and analysis.

- Adaptive security systems that learn and evolve based on emerging threats.

2. Zero Trust Security Models:

- Moving away from traditional perimeter-based security.

- Implementing a "never trust, always verify" approach to user and device access.

3. Quantum Computing Threats and Defenses:

- Anticipating the impact of quantum computing on current encryption methods.

- Developing quantum-resistant encryption algorithms.

4. Rise of Cyber-Physical Security:

- Increased focus on securing the Internet of Things (IoT) devices.

- Ensuring the security of interconnected systems in critical infrastructure.

5. Extended Detection and Response (XDR):

- Integration of multiple security components for more comprehensive threat detection and response.

- Providing a unified view of security across endpoints, networks, and cloud environments.

6. Cloud Security Evolution:

- Continued emphasis on securing cloud-based infrastructure and services.

- Integration of security into DevOps processes (DevSecOps).

7. 5G Security Challenges:

- Addressing security concerns related to the widespread adoption of 5G technology.

- Ensuring the confidentiality and integrity of data transmitted over 5G networks.

8. Biometric Authentication Advances:

- Growing use of biometrics for user authentication.

- Addressing privacy and security concerns associated with biometric data.

9. Blockchain for Cybersecurity:

- Exploring the use of blockchain for secure transactions and data integrity.

- Potential applications in identity management and secure communication.

10. Human-Centric Security:

- Recognizing the role of human factors in cybersecurity.

- Investing in user education and awareness programs.

11. **Regulatory Compliance and Privacy:**

   - Continued focus on data protection regulations (e.g., GDPR, CCPA).

   - Adapting cybersecurity practices to comply with evolving legal frameworks.

12. **Automated Threat Hunting:**

   - Leveraging automation for proactive threat hunting and response.

   - Analyzing large datasets to identify patterns and potential threats.

13. **Cybersecurity Workforce Development:**

   - Addressing the shortage of skilled cybersecurity professionals.

   - Investing in training and educational programs.

Conclusion

As we near the end of our voyage through the complex environment of advanced penetration testing, it becomes evident that cybersecurity is more than simply an area of study; it is a constant war against emerging threats. Mastering the art of cyber resilience is not a luxury in the digital arena, where attackers are as smart as the technologies they use.

We descended into the depths of network vulnerabilities, exploited the complexities of online applications, and comprehended the nuances of developing technologies during our investigation. However, our goal was not only to comprehend the complexities of offensive techniques; it was to equip you, the reader, to become a digital fortress protector.

As you close the final chapter, remember that knowledge is the greatest armour against cyber threats. Each line you've read, each technique you've learned, is a shield against potential breaches. But beyond the tools and methodologies lies a responsibility—to wield this knowledge ethically and contribute to the collective defence of our interconnected world.

The journey does not end here; it transforms. Take this newfound wisdom and apply it with integrity. Let it be a force for good, a beacon in the ever-changing landscape of cybersecurity. Whether you are a seasoned professional or a curious enthusiast, the power to safeguard our digital future is now in your hands.

As we bid farewell to these pages, let them serve as a reminder that in the realm of cybersecurity, there are no final victories—only persistent defences. Stay vigilant, stay informed, and let the principles of ethical hacking guide your path. Together, we can fortify the virtual realms we inhabit and ensure that the digital landscape remains secure for generations to come.

Thank you for embarking on this journey. May your endeavours in the realm of cybersecurity be marked by resilience, integrity, and an unwavering commitment to safeguarding the digital world.

—-